The Old Convent
East Grinstead

John Mason Neale, George Edmund Street
and the Society of St Margaret

Kathryn Ferry

Published by the Old Convent Estate Residents Limited to mark the 150th anniversary of the opening of the former St Margaret's Convent, East Grinstead.

The Old Convent Estate Residents Limited,
Crown House, 37 High Street, East Grinstead RH19 3AF
oldconventestate@gmail.com

First published in Great Britain in 2021

Designer Robin Stannard
Project Manager Cindy Scott Clark
Printed and bound in Great Britain by Page Brothers, Norwich

Copyright © The Old Convent Estate Residents Limited and Dr Kathryn Ferry

Dr Kathryn Ferry has asserted her rights under the Copyright, Designs and Patents Act, 1988 to be identified as the author of this work

Photographs of original G E Street drawings are all © RIBA Collections and may not be reproduced. Those published here were taken by the author. In the exceptional circumstances of the Coronavirus pandemic throughout 2020 professional photography by RIBA staff was not possible.

All rights reserved. No parts of this publication may be reproduced or transmitted in any form or by any means, electronic or mechanical, including photocopying, recording, or any information retrieval systems without prior permission in writing from the publishers

ISBN 978-1-5272-8952-9

Figure 1 *The capacious interior of G E Street's chapel. A covenant means that this spectacular space can never be altered.*

Contents

Acknowledgements	6
Foreword by Elizabeth Williamson	8
Introduction	9
Chapter One The Society of St Margaret	13
The Oxford Movement and early Anglican Sisterhoods	14
John Mason Neale and the Society of St Margaret	18
Lewes Riot: Cause and Effect	30
St Margaret's Home	33
Chapter Two A Purpose-built Convent	41
The Gothic Revival and the Cambridge Camden Society	43
G E Street and the Design for St Margaret's	50
Laying the Foundation Stone	61
Chapter Three The Progress of Works	69
Phase One: 1865-74	70
Funding	90
Phase Two: 1878-1900	95
Chapter Four Convent Life	**109**
Living at St Margaret's	110
Nursing and Mission Work	119
Ecclesiastical Art	130
Chapter Five The Orphanage and Schools	**143**
St Margaret's Orphanage and the Industrials	144
The Convent Schools – St Agnes', St Margaret's and St Michael's	156
Chapter Six Change and Legacy	**173**
Timeline	182
Notes	184
Bibliography	190
Picture Credits	194

Acknowledgements

I became interested in the Society of St Margaret after being commissioned to write a conservation report about their first premises on Church Lane. As a scholar of Victorian architecture I'd been fascinated by the Old Convent since moving to East Grinstead in 2007 and after being given a tour by Julie Goode I was thrilled that she thought the idea of a book on its history would be welcomed by residents. Julie and David Goode have been great supporters of the project and deserve huge thanks, as do Will and Susan Quekett for all their hard work seeing it through, and Simon and Sally Fishburne who have known and loved the buildings for nearly forty years.

It has also been a privilege to have the co-operation of St Margaret's Convent, together with the help and support of Sr Sarah SSM. At Sackville College I could not have done without the unfailing assistance of Rosalind Crowther and Caroline Metcalfe, Warden and Historian respectively. Anna James and Jessica Woodward, librarians at Pusey House, have kindly answered my questions and shared material from the wonderful SSM collection there. Thanks also go to Elizabeth Williamson for writing the Foreword, Geoff Brandwood for insights on the Gothic Revival, John Goodall for making me think again about architectural sources, Alex Bremner for help with Ecclesiologist queries, the Right Reverend Dominic Walker OGS for comments on the first draft, Sarah Sexton for stained glass advice, Jonathan Parrett of East Grinstead Museum and Steve Metcalfe, Marcus Bryant and Linda Bryant at Sackville College, Richard and Karen Dandy of Spires Hairdressing.

For their help with illustrations thanks go to the Reverend Canon Myles Davies of Liverpool Cathedral, Simon Batten at Bloxham School, Sr Judith SSM, Holy Priory, Hackney, York

Minster Heritage Team, the staff of the RIBA drawings collection at the V&A and those at the Paul Mellon Centre. Cindy Scott-Clark and Robin Stannard have done a fantastic job with the design and the beautiful photography by Will Pryce absolutely lifts the book. For creating the stunning videos that support and promote the book special thanks are also due to Lindsay Lowe and Zoe Lewin of Duck Productions. Anne and Mike Murray gave me useful information about Cricket Court and I am also grateful to Alexander Samoilove and to all the Old Convent residents who I hope will enjoy reading their book as much as I've enjoyed writing it. For their valuable proofreading help, my special thanks go to Sara Brennan, Vanessa Ferry and Matthew Slocombe.

Foreword

A revision of the West Sussex part of Nairn and Pevsner's *The Buildings of England: Sussex* brought me to the Old Convent, nearly fifty years after that guide was published. Though the original pastoral setting has gone, the silhouette – rising to the chapel's noble tower – perfectly captures the spirit of romance that the convent's founder, John Mason Neale, sensed would attract worshippers to a revived Church of England. As Kathryn Ferry, author of this absorbing study, says 'Romanticism provided the cultural backdrop to this renewed interest in Gothic architecture.' What makes the Old Convent so special is the way in which the architect, G E Street, convincingly married medieval architecture with the practical planning needed for daily life by the Anglican nuns for whom he was designing. And the story of those nuns, the pioneering and exceptionally gifted members of the Society of St Margaret, is a revelation. The range and professionalism of their skills – chiefly nursing, teaching, and embroidery – and the management and dissemination of them shows Victorian women in a new and truer light. Thanks to Kathryn's research and to the residents' support for it, future visitors and custodians of the Old Convent will be enriched by knowledge of its special history, from the ideals of its conception and the difficulties in funding its protracted construction to the industrious and religious life that went on within its walls.

Elizabeth Williamson

Co-author of *The Buildings of England. Sussex: West*, Yale University Press (London 2019)

April 2020

Introduction

The former St Margaret's Convent is arguably the most important building in East Grinstead. Its Grade I listing places the convent in England's top 2.5% of all historic structures. This designation reflects the fact that it was designed by an architect of national significance as the Mother House for an order of nuns whose charitable mission still operates on an international stage.

At the start of Queen Victoria's reign established religion was challenged by the so-called Oxford Movement, which sought to reinstate elements of Catholic worship into the Church of England following the Catholic Emancipation Act of 1829. This High Church Anglo-Catholicism went hand-in-hand with the Gothic Revival in church architecture. It also encompassed the establishment of monastic communities which had not been allowed within the Anglican Church since the Dissolution three hundred years earlier.

Thanks to the Industrial Revolution, Victorian Britain had become the powerhouse of the world but the great wealth generated by industrialists masked terrible inequalities and dire poverty. When the only safety net to catch the poorest in society was the workhouse, it fell to philanthropists and Christian campaigners to fight for those who had no voice themselves. Sisterhoods were a response to this need but they also fulfilled an important role in providing upper and middle class women with valid work at a time when their sphere was being increasingly confined to a domestic setting.

St Margaret's was not alone in being established by a man though in other cases where this happened tensions rapidly developed between the founder's aims and the goals of the all-female community. John Mason Neale was no ordinary man, however, and his dedication to the spiritual well-being of the women who joined his Sisterhood was repaid by their devotion to his example of tireless commitment to the mission. *The Guardian's* obituary of Neale remarked how 'Those who are familiar with the aspect and demeanour of the East Grinstead Sisters have often been struck with their conspicuous buoyancy and cheerfulness, contrasting so forcibly with the popular idea of the morbid depression supposed to be inseparable from the life of a Sister of Mercy.'[1]

Founded in 1854, by 1883 St Margaret's was the largest Anglican religious house in England.[2] Following Neale's premature death in 1866 the convent became his memorial. In *The Call of the Cloister*, Peter Anson described it as 'an example of Gothic Revival architecture which no other country in Europe can equal.'[3]

This book tells the story of how the Society of St Margaret came to be created, how major doubts about their motives were dispelled by the Sisters' selfless desire to help others and how they created a community that put East Grinstead on the map. It also examines the architectural history of their convent and its place within the wider Gothic Revival as a key building in the oeuvre of George Edmund Street. It describes how the buildings were designed, erected and used until the Sisters moved to new premises in 1976 and concludes with an assessment of the convent's impact and legacy.

Figure 2 *Watercolour view looking towards the lodge and chapel from Moat Road.*

Figure 3 *The courtyard of St Margaret's Home, Church Lane painted by a member of the community in the 1860s.*

Chapter 1
The Society of St Margaret

The Oxford Movement and early Anglican Sisterhoods

There was a palpable feeling of social change in the 1830s. Government was compelled into creating a fairer electoral system after rioting demonstrated the urgency of the 1832 Reform Act and the concept of workers' rights made its first tentative appearance with the regulation of children's employment in cotton mills. At the same time, however, conditions for the unemployed were debased as the New Poor Law Act of 1834 set out a punitive approach to poverty, sanctioning worse conditions in the workhouse than those a poor labourer would find outside. In Britain's religious life, the passing of the 1829 Catholic Emancipation Act opened up a space for debate about the future of the Church of England and its role in national life.

At Oxford University, a group of academics and clerics, grouped around John Keble became increasingly outspoken about the needs and shortcomings of the contemporary church. After July 1833, when Keble gave his Assize Sermon on National Apostasy, questioning how far the State should have control over the Church, their protests coalesced and the Oxford Movement was born. Under the editorship of John Henry Newman, Vicar of the University Church of St Mary the Virgin, a series of *Tracts for the Times* was begun to question modern worship and promote a return to the pre-Reformation Catholic heritage of the Church of England. Publication of these ninety tracts earned supporters the name of Tractarians but they were also known as Newmanites and Puseyites, the latter after Edward Bouverie Pusey who emerged as the Movement's new figurehead in the 1840s.

Controversy dogged the Movement but this did not stop it making major inroads into the national consciousness. The Tractarian focus on theology was combined with a great revival of interest in liturgy and church architecture, led in no small part by the Cambridge Camden Society, co-founded in 1839 by John Mason Neale, of which more will be said in the next chapter. In parish churches around the country newly-graduated clerics began putting the Movement's High Church ideals into practice. These men, dubbed 'Ritualists', attracted a disproportionately high percentage of women to their congregations. Some critics claimed that the more decorative Gothic atmosphere of Oxford Movement churches explained this appeal but there were other reasons too.

All exponents of the Anglo-Catholic Revival insisted upon the need for active work and charity, both as a form of spiritual discipline and to obey the commands of Christ. This call applied equally to women and men. Figures from the census show that from 1851 onwards there were more women than men in the British population, a fact which had serious implications for a society that prioritised marriage as the only path to female happiness. Church work could be used to fill the empty hours of middle-aged spinsters who would otherwise be judged as objects of pity, it could give young women with greater aspirations a purpose and it could make middle class wives whose servants did everything for them, feel truly useful. As John Shelton Reed has put it, 'by providing idle women with occupations, however humble, it implied they had contributions to make'.[4] For a theological movement with outwardly traditional and conservative aims providing such an opportunity for female emancipation was paradoxically radical yet demonstrably welcome.

The logical extension of this principle was the establishment of Anglican sisterhoods. During the Dissolution of the monasteries King Henry VIII had banned monks and nuns, taking their property for the State. In the early nineteenth century, however, the poet Robert Southey resurrected the idea of sisterhoods suggesting they could fulfil a dual purpose as refuge for

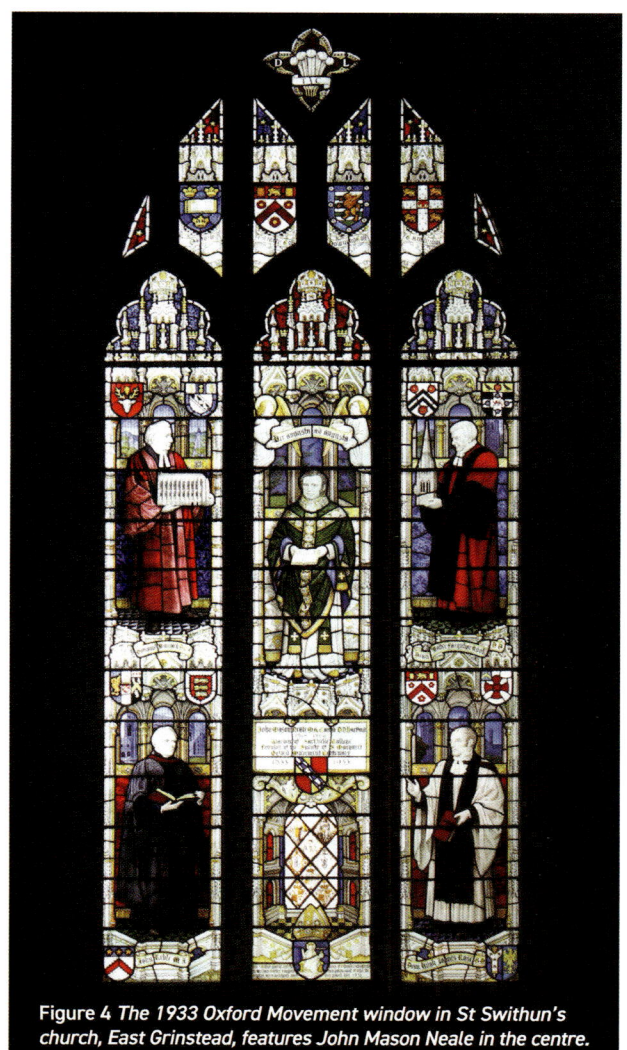

Figure 4 *The 1933 Oxford Movement window in St Swithun's church, East Grinstead, features John Mason Neale in the centre.*

Figure 5 *This 1866 Punch cartoon satirises the perceived femininity of 'The Ritual Movement'. A parcel of vestments ordered by high church clergyman 'the Reverend Augustine Cope' is waylaid by his pretty cousins who use it for dressing up.*

unmarried women and social resource for the care of the poor. Dr Pusey gathered together a committee of prominent men to bring this goal about and in Easter Week 1845, he opened a small house near Regent's Park from which the first modern Sisters of Mercy would operate.

Members of the Sisterhood of the Holy Cross, otherwise known as Park Village, set to work in the slums of Somers Town and Camden but their lack of strong female leadership soon became a problem. In 1856 they were absorbed into Ascot Priory (the Society of

Most Holy Trinity) which had been founded by Priscilla Lydia Sellon in 1848, to answer the Bishop of Exeter's call for gentlewomen to work among the poor and sick of Devonport and Plymouth. Despite Sellon's ritualistic practices and autocratic style making her enemies, her influence on the burgeoning sisterhood movement was profound.

Other important early sisterhoods included the Community of Saint Mary the Virgin, established in 1848 at Wantage by the Vicar William John Butler and run, from 1850 to 1887, by Harriet Day, the daughter of a Sussex farmer. Her role as Superior, won by talent rather than social class, encouraged other intelligent and ambitious women to join. Notwithstanding this example, sisterhoods generally maintained outside divisions by designating wealthy women as Choir sisters, able to make significant financial contributions to the community, and Lay sisters who could not. That sisterhoods held a real allure among upper class women is clear from the fact that many founders were drawn from that strata of society.

The nursing Community of All Saints may have been established in the slums of Marylebone but it was the brainchild of the 'immensely rich' Harriet Brownlow Byron, daughter of a former MP and Deputy Lieutenant of Hertfordshire. The Community of St John the Baptist, at Clewer, also founded in 1851, was created near the Windsor military camp to provide a refuge and penitentiary for prostitutes. Established by Harriet Monsell, the daughter of an Irish MP and baronet, it was considered one of the most fashionable sisterhoods, with the ability to attract members of the aristocratic elite. In 1869 Penelope Holland warned that 'in the present day there is scarcely any alternative for a girl in fashionable society, between reckless dissipation and a convent life. The latter is being chosen oftener year by year.'[5]

Research by Susan Mumm has shown that between 1845 and 1900 more than ninety sisterhoods were formed within the Anglican Church. Some women stayed a few months only to realise the life was not for them; others did not leave until their death. In all, some 10,000 women passed through these communities in the first fifty-five years.[6]

John Mason Neale and the Society of St Margaret

That one of the largest sisterhoods was established in East Grinstead was the direct result of John Mason Neale's residence there, as Warden of Sackville College. Sister Kate was among the earliest recruits and her memoirs provide one of the best sources for the community in its pre-Convent days. She describes East Grinstead in the 1840s as indistinct from other Sussex towns, 'a sleepy, old-fashioned place.' It was, she said, 'deeply impregnated – as were most old country towns at that time – with its own conservative prejudices, manners and customs.' Into this came Neale: 'Young, ardent, enthusiastic, large-hearted, full of sympathy, a poet, a scholar, a student, and to crown all, gifted with intense energy of purpose, never, to our judgement, did man seem more utterly out of place than was this young Priest, in the midst of these surroundings.'[7]

John Mason Neale was born on 24 January 1818 at 40 Lamb's Conduit Street, London, the first child and only son of the Rev. Cornelius Neale and his wife, Susanna Good. The family were strongly Evangelical though Neale was not an average clergyman, having pursued his love of literature and the theatre before seeking ordination in 1820. Four years

Figure 6 *Studio portrait of John Mason Neale in his cassock.*

previously he had married Susanna, the daughter of John Mason Good, a London doctor with linguistic and literary talents. After Cornelius Neale died prematurely in 1823 his widow moved frequently for the sake of her health ensuring a somewhat itinerant childhood for her son and three younger daughters. Despite this John Mason Neale distinguished himself by his academic abilities. In 1836 he won a scholarship to Trinity College, Cambridge.

After a successful first year of studying Neale spent part of his summer vacation with Edward Boyce at St Leonards, near Hastings. The friends made a tour of churches in the neighbourhood beginning a practice of church visiting that was to inspire Neale's campaign to improve ecclesiastical art and architecture. As Neale's biographer A G Lough declared; 'Within the next few years he was to show a remarkable development, and whilst still an undergraduate he was to become in effect the

Figure 7 *The entrance front of Sackville College.*

leader of the Catholic revival in the Church of England at Cambridge and later to direct it into new channels.'[8] In May 1839, with Boyce and another lifelong friend Benjamin Webb, he founded the Cambridge Camden (later Ecclesiological) Society which was to influence 'the concept and fabric of Victorian churches throughout Britain and the colonies.'[9]

In 1841 Neale was ordained a deacon, becoming a priest the following year. His radical views made finding employment difficult; he resigned from the post of chaplain at Downing College within weeks while his attempt to become a curate at Guildford was scuppered when the Evangelical Bishop of Winchester refused him a licence. Offered the living of Crawley in May 1842, Neale happily envisaged the creation of a model parish there with his soon-to-be-wife Sarah Webster. This was not to be as a diagnosis of consumption required that he travel abroad for a healthier climate. After their wedding on 27 July 1842 Neale and his wife set out for the first of three life-saving visits to Madeira. With his health steadily improving he returned to his writing, which, over the course of his life was to encompass works for clergy and laity, adults and children. In his mission to improve readers' understanding of Christian history, Anglican theology and liturgical practice he harnessed history, fiction, biography, sermons, travelogues and poetry, both original and in translation.

By the time that Neale heard of the vacancy for a Warden at Sackville College in January 1846 he was ready to take on a new job. Though the charitable statutes of the almshouse, founded by the second earl of Dorset in 1608, did not stipulate a clerical appointment the patrons, Lady De La Warr and her husband, the fifth earl, were pleased to employ Neale and remained his staunch supporters through the many difficulties he had to face whilst in post. First of these was the inhibition imposed upon Neale by the Bishop of Chichester in 1847 which stopped him from celebrating or performing *any* clerical functions in the diocese. It had been Neale's renovation of the sadly neglected chapel at Sackville College that prompted this move by the bishop and though Neale and his supporters argued the chapel was outside the diocesan authority they lost the case. Local opposition to his brand of Anglo-Catholicism could be fierce, not least when hysterically whipped up by the Brighton Protestant Association and its mouthpiece the *Brighton Gazette.*

Figure 8 *Early 19th century oil painting of East Grinstead from the Lewes Road. The gables of Sackville College can be seen next to the church tower with typical Sussex cottages in the foreground.*

This opposition was most forcibly demonstrated in March 1851 when Neale's attempts to reform funeral practices provoked a riot along East Grinstead High Street. Until this point it had been customary for the coffin to be carried on men's shoulders; as they braced their heads against the box they joined arms or hands underneath. Over both the coffin and the bearers a black pall was thrown which made it impossible for the men to see where they were going. Neale replaced the bearers with a wheeled bier and laid a purple pall on the coffin with a plain cross on it. Such was the novelty of this arrangement that crowds came to see it, alarming the local Vicar who took it as clear evidence of Neale's Roman leanings. The inmates of Sackville College were required to consent to this new form of funeral as a condition of their residence but the relatives of Mrs Aulchin, though *she* had consented, objected in the most violent way. On the day of her burial they came to the College with an unruly mob and demanded the coffin which they then proceeded to open in a local inn to verify the presence of the body. Around 150 people, dressed up in disguise and carrying 'torches, firepans, oil, shavings, straw and other combustibles' returned to the College where they burnt a bier, a pall and crosses in the field, smashed windows and lit a fire against the side of the house where Neale's children were lying seriously ill in bed. During the three hour long riot both Neale and his wife were also physically attacked.[10] That no one came to their aid speaks volumes about how they were viewed by the townspeople. After this Neale did not dare venture into East Grinstead after dark.

And yet, three years later he began making plans for the even more controversial establishment of an Anglican Sisterhood. A man of remarkable character, Neale was not to be deterred by potential opposition. His personal motto was 'What is possible *may* be done; what is impossible *must* be done.'[11]

Neale had been thinking about the benefits of reintroducing monastic life for a long time and had revealed his position as early as 1843 in his swiftly penned second novel *Ayton Priory*. Though this was merely idle speculation, since his move to East Grinstead he had become painfully aware of the problem of rural poverty. Sister Kate recalled how:

> Running around the gable of the Warden's house, outside the College, is a flagged path, which commands a view of the whole countryside. Below the town lies a green belt of pasture-land, beyond which the brown ridges of Ashdown Forest sweep the southern horizon, and on clear days the distant purple of Crowborough Beacon is visible...Beautiful as this lovely view is to look at, scattered over the vast area, buried in the woods and out of the way wilds, were innumerable hamlets and isolated cottages, badly built, badly drained, far from human help and resource, when fever or any illness attacked the inmates. Day after day, as he paced, as his custom was, up and down this terrace, and looked out over the fair scene, his heart burned within him at the thought of all the miseries of these wretched cottages hidden away among the wilds.[12]

Figure 9 *Mother Ann wearing the grey habit of St Margaret's. The size of her cross and the unusual ruff worn around her neck may have been the marks of her status as Superior.*

The two things came together one rainy November day in 1853 as he sat staring out of his study window; 'it flashed into my mind, "If I could but have women for that work!"' A few days later he mentioned the idea to Miss Ann Gream who gave the most encouraging words possible 'Why not have a Sisterhood here? – and I will belong to it.'[13]

The urgent need was for nurses to tend the poor in their own homes. In the mid-nineteenth century healthcare provision was in its infancy, doctors had to be paid for and nursing was yet to be viewed as a reputable occupation. Florence Nightingale commented that nursing was done by those 'who were too old, too weak, too drunken, too dirty, too stolid, or too bad to do anything else.'[14] Neale was aware that a local priest named Fowler had floated the idea of nurses 'trained both physically and religiously' before the Rural Deanery in 1850 but no action was taken. He knew too, that a single woman could do 'incalculable good work' since he had frequently come into contact with the daughter of a master-bricklayer at Horley who had been partially trained as a nurse at Oxford. Neale's reputation as a writer and his profile within the Anglo-Catholic community meant that he had already been approached by three women seeking advice about joining a Sisterhood.[15] They would become the nucleus of his experiment.

To ensure the greatest chance of success Neale canvassed his friends for support then visited the Sisterhood at Clewer where he found a workable model for the rules by which his Sisters would live and an important ally in the Mother Superior. After Britain entered the Crimean War in March 1854 press reports of insanitary conditions in Turkish medical stations saw nursing climb the political agenda and, capitalising on this, Neale wrote to clergy and gentry in the Diocese asking first for support and then funds. Both were forthcoming so by the end of the year the first Sisters were able to move into Sackville College where they cared for sick inmates and began their spiritual training with the Warden.

Faith and devotion were critically important to aid the Sisters in the difficult tasks ahead but Neale also realised that they needed the best medical training they could get. After negotiations with Sussex County Hospital failed, Neale met enthusiasm for his project among the physicians at Westminster Hospital who agreed to provide two-month training places for his Sisters.[16] Sister Ellen (born Ellen Horner at Ibstone, Oxfordshire c1825, a widow) was the first to go in February 1855, followed after

Figure 10 *The substantial rectory at Rotherfield which Mother Ann left to take up her calling.*

Easter by Sister Alice (born Alice Jenny Crocker at Woburn, Bedfordshire c1830). A third Sister, who was not named because she lacked the social status of a 'lady', was then residing at Rotherfield 'with her Superior.'[17] A handwritten list of Sisters held in the library of Sackville College shows that this was Sister Elizabeth, the first Lay Sister, professed in October 1855. The widow of a Newfoundland missionary, Sister Elizabeth appears to have felt her calling so strongly that she left her children in order to join the Sisterhood. She died on 29 August 1860, most likely as a result of contagion from cottage nursing.[18]

The experience of other Sisterhoods proved the importance of finding the right Mother Superior and Neale's invitation to Ann Gream came early in the planning process. She was, he wrote, 'the very exact person of all others I could have chosen, just about the right age – forty-five; used all her life to parish works; used to nursing, and most anxious to be employed in some way.'[19] Born Sarah Ann Gream c1809 at Godstone in Kent (now Surrey) she took her vows to become Mother Ann in June 1855. It was she who chose to dedicate the Sisterhood to St Margaret of Antioch, one of the most venerated saints of the medieval period.

Mother Ann came from a strongly religious family. Her widowed father was rector of Rotherfield, her brother was rector of Springfield near Chelmsford and her younger sister Katherine Ann Gream became another pioneer in Anglican sisterhoods, taking on the role of first Mother Superior at the community of St Mary's in Brighton from 1858 until her death in 1873. Neale was good friends with 'old Gream' and recorded that he 'entered heartily into the [Sisterhood] plan', so much so that he was prepared to put his own name to a statement sent out to 210 local parishes explaining how the new nurses would operate.[20] Neither Neale's name nor the Sisterhood were mentioned for fear of being too divisive. Mr Gream, however, was elderly and in frail health so Mother Ann's acceptance of the post was contingent on her being able to nurse her father in his final days. For this reason a small house was taken in Rotherfield which effectively became the first base for the Sisterhood, a place where the Sisters could live when they were not out nursing in the local area.

On Easter Day 1855 the Sisters came out in their distinctive habit for the first time. Prior to this they had simply worn whatever black clothes they had. Conscious of its association

Figure 11 *1960s photograph of Sackville College from the church tower. The large red brick building (bottom right) is no. 8 Church Lane. The former carriage house by its side was converted to an oratory by G F Bodley.*

with mourning and 'because the poor have so often a prejudice against a nurse in black', the Sisters chose a grey uniform.[21] They thought children would prefer the softer tone too though the novelty of their costume probably overwhelmed any fears about colour. It was 300 years since nuns had been common in Britain and nothing like these communities had existed within living memory. Though they were now on the increase they must have been a startling sight in rural Sussex. The simplicity and lack of shape in their garb was also a huge contrast to the nipped-in corset waists and full-skirted crinolines then in fashion. Leaving behind the colour and frills of normal clothing, ladies who joined a Sisterhood gained an unusual degree of independence in exchange. To their starched white headgear they attached a veil for worship that was also worn when they went out. This habit defined them as different, allowing them to set their own rules, travelling alone and working in social situations that would otherwise have been closed to them.

To really establish his Sisterhood Neale needed more women to sign up so in February 1855 he wrote to Mrs Sidney Herbert, wife of the War Secretary. It was her husband, 1st Baron Herbert of Lea, who had charged Florence Nightingale to lead a party of nurses to improve conditions at the military hospital in Scutari (in modern Istanbul). Mrs Herbert managed the recruitment of nurses at home and she agreed to supply Neale with lists of women who were unsuitable to go to the Crimea (because they were below the age of thirty and therefore considered too young) but who might suit St Margaret's. It is unclear whether new Sisters joined by this route but the lodgings at Rotherfield could not accommodate many more and it was soon apparent that a more permanent home was required.

Cottage nursing proved extremely strenuous work. The society's first case involved caring for Mrs Bridger who was dying of tuberculosis in a run-down cottage at Saxonbury Hill, about five miles from Tunbridge Wells. Between 13 July 1855 and the patient's death in March 1856, Sister Alice and Sister Ellen took it in turns to live in the loft of a nearby cottage, looking after Mrs Bridger but also undertaking all the normal household chores that she could not: taking care of the baby, mending clothes, dressing the young children, cooking, cleaning and, throughout the winter, fetching firewood from the forest. The Sisters lived like the poor they attended and so wretched were their circumstances that Neale's

Figure 12 *Mrs Bridger's cottage at Woodside, sketched by one of the sisters who nursed there. The Bridger family occupied the tiled part only so the sisters had to sleep in a nearby cottage which had holes in the thatch above where they slept.*

spiritual counsel was crucial for their ability to go on. He visited as frequently as he could and wrote almost daily. When there was no other means of transport he walked the fourteen miles each way to Rotherfield but the problem of distance came to a head when Neale suffered a very bad carriage accident in February 1856.

For the community to prosper it needed to be closer to its founder. With the death of Mr Gream that spring the Mother Superior and her Sisters were finally able to move into new premises at No. 8 Church Lane, East Grinstead. On 28 April 1856 Neale wrote of it to his friend Benjamin Webb:

> Now we have taken a house here- close to the College- between it and the Church. A red brick building of 1753, ugly enough, but not offensive. It will hold twelve sisters well. What is the present house at Rotherfield, we turn into a Cottage Hospital. The house is taken from Midsummer.[22]

In Sister Gabriel's account of the convent's history she describes the building as 'small and very barely furnished, but full of joy, hope and desire for total giving.'[23] By September 1856 the number of Sisters had risen to nine.

A little building to the north of the house, previously used for storing a pony chaise, was converted into their private chapel or oratory by architect George Frederick Bodley (1827-1907). Like his friend G E Street, Bodley was a former pupil of George Gilbert Scott (1811-78) and though this was a very small commission it was nonetheless important in church history. In this humble building, outside the jurisdiction of Anglican authority, Neale reintroduced controversial liturgical practices; specifically the daily Eucharist in 1856 and, for probably the first time in the Church of England in the nineteenth century, the Reservation of the Blessed Sacrament in 1857. The Sisters followed the Catholic belief that consecrated sacramental bread and wine were changed into the veritable body and blood of Jesus Christ during the liturgy of Eucharist. The practice of Reservation, by which a portion of the consecrated elements is set aside and reserved after the reception of communion, was previously unheard of in the Anglican Church but its original purpose, to allow the blessed sacrament to be taken to the ill, homebound or dying, had a clear application to the Sister's mission. Despite this logic, anti-Catholic feeling was such that it had to be kept secret from those outside the Sisterhood.[24]

The Lewes Riot: Cause and Effect

As the Sisters continued their nursing and were called upon to go further afield, respect and admiration for their work increased. This did not, however, sway bigoted Protestants in the locality whose number included the assistant wardens at Sackville College, as well as the vicar of East Grinstead who preached a sermon against Popery on the Sunday after the nuns moved into their new home opposite St Swithun's Church. Sister Kate wrote that Neale had 'not the slightest Roman tastes or tendencies: no man less'.[25] His preference was to return the English Church to its pre-Reformation heritage but the finer points of the debate were lost on people who only saw the outward signs of greater ceremonial and felt their own religious views under threat. This was very much part of a nationwide stirring of anti-Catholic feeling exacerbated by press reports in the wake of the re-institution of Catholic bishops in 1850.

In this context the choice to become an Anglo-Catholic nun must be understood as a very brave one. To bind the community together Neale developed a daily routine of worship that was 'his own particular brand of tradition mingled with innovation...' The monastic Offices set a framework for their daily prayer, centred around the Blessed Sacrament. They also loved and revered the Holy Name of Jesus, treating everyone they cared for equally in the spirit of His words "Inasmuch as ye have done it unto one of the least of these ye have done it unto Me". In addition Neale encouraged the prayerful study of the Bible, leading by example.[26] This was the structured and unifying life that nurtured the Sisters in between bouts of nursing and it was this that helped them endure the extreme poverty, squalor and danger of death they faced with every new case. In the first year there was an outbreak of scarlet fever among the Sisters in which Mother Ann nearly died and three others were desperately ill.

The tragic story of Sister Amy, who succumbed to scarlet fever in 1857, demonstrates not only the risks taken by these women, but also the way in which they were viewed as defying conventional femininity. Embracing a radical religious ideology, the women who chose this life were young feminists, seeking an alternative path to the prescribed course of marriage and motherhood. It was a fact not lost on their detractors and, combined with the strength of anti-Catholic hatred, proved a heady mix that threatened the very future of St Margaret's.

Sister Amy was the eldest daughter of the Rev John Scobell, the low church Rector of Southover and All Saints', Lewes. Born Emily Ann Elizabeth Scobell, she had been a delicate child and, until the birth of her first brother when she was ten, her father's favourite. This made it all the harder for him to accept her interest in Tractarian teaching, which she had first encountered around the age of eighteen. Though Neale recorded she had been the 'belle of Lewes races and assize balls' Emily was already reading his books and rebelling against the life her father had planned for her.[27] Without her father's knowledge Emily met Neale in February 1855 and made her first confession to him. His acquiescence in this secrecy was later to rebound heavily on Neale who was accused by Scobell of poisoning his daughter's mind against her family. Emily repeatedly asked her father's permission to go to East Grinstead and test her vocation but he steadfastly refused. We might presume that as a thirty-year old woman she knew her own mind and had the right to choose but this was not so in the mid-nineteenth century. In common with most middle class fathers Scobell expected his daughter to remain as his carer if she did not find a husband to whose alternate authority she could submit. When Emily failed to return from a prolonged visit to the West Country she wrote to inform her father that, on 15 August 1857, she had entered St Margaret's and assumed the title of Sister Amy.

Figure 13 *The cross erected in memory of Sister Amy was moved from its original location on Church Lane to the convent quadrangle in 1870 where it still stands.*

The rancour caused by this mode of parting might have cooled over time but it was all too fresh in Scobell's mind when his daughter died, having contracted scarlet fever a mere month after joining the Sisterhood. In his diary of this period Neale wrote of how Sister Amy often professed her astonishment at events: 'How strange that I should so long have wished to enter a Sisterhood, and should only have entered one to die there!'[28] She insisted upon making a will, appointing Neale and Mother Ann as executors. The majority of her estate, worth some £5-6,000, was bequeathed to her brother with £400 left to the Sisterhood. As death drew nearer she asked to see her father but, though the message was sent, he failed to arrive in time to make peace with his daughter before she passed away on Friday 13 November.

At her own request, Sister Amy was buried with her mother in the family vault at All Saints. Her father specified that the service be held at 5.30pm meaning that the churchyard was dark when the funeral procession, including Neale and eight of the Sisters, arrived from the station. A mob gathered outside the church, whose 'uproar, hooting and yelling' Neale considered to be 'most evidently preconcerted.' As the family moved into the vault for the burial on the north side of the churchyard, the lights were extinguished and the nuns were set upon by the rabble. Neither Scobell nor the apparent 'gentlemen' there gathered made any attempt to assist as the 'ladies were dashed this way and that, their veils dragged off and their dresses torn.'[29] Some of the Sisters took refuge in the Schoolmaster's house, others in the King's Head pub. By this time the mob was reckoned to be 3,000 strong. Neale himself escaped through gardens and over two 9ft high walls to the station and home.

The Lewes Riot was reported nationally with both Neale and Scobell putting their side of the story to the people through newspapers and pamphlets. The latter actually claimed that his daughter, 'an overwrought, dissatisfied, and disobedient child', had been purposely exposed to illness in order that the Sisterhood could take her money.[30] Magnifying this claim a lurid pamphlet was subsequently published under the title: *Painful Account of the Perversion and Untimely Death of Miss Scobell, the Stolen Daughter of the Revd. J. Scobell, inveigled from her home, persuaded to become a Puseyite Sister of Mercy and through threats of eternal damnation to her soul, plundered of her property by a crafty band of Puseyite Jesuits for the support of Popery.* This was a new level of notoriety for John Mason Neale who wrote to his friend that 'it is not pleasant to be posted over England as a rascal.'³¹ Worse still was the impact upon the Sisterhood which saw donations cease, subscriptions drop and high profile support withdrawn, most especially from the Bishop of Chichester who had been Visitor of the Community. In East Grinstead, the dissenting landlord of No. 8 Church Lane, gave the Sisters notice to quit.

St Margaret's Home

Despite such significant setbacks Neale and the Sisters continued to believe that their faith and good works would provide a solution. This proved to be true after a lady witnessed Mother Ann nursing a sick man in East Grinstead and persuaded her employer, a currier called Mr Felton, for whom she acted as housekeeper, to let one of his vacant properties to the Sisterhood. The location could not have been more perfect, just along Church Lane from their first home and still next to Sackville College. They moved in to No. 1 Church Lane, now Spires Hairdressing, on Midsummer's Day 1858. Once again G F Bodley was called in to make the necessary architectural alterations. Later that summer Katherine Anne Egerton Warburton, the daughter of a Tractarian vicar

born in 1840, came to East Grinstead from her family home in Cheshire. Aged eighteen, she adopted the name of Sister Kate and later recalled her first impressions:

> A funny little home it was, standing endwise to the road, approached by a flight of brick steps, shut in by a door from the causeway outside. Inside, a tiny hall, screened from the staircase by a red baize curtain; in the left the door opened into the Mother's room, which looked across the road on to the churchyard – an ecclesiastical room, with texts and plainly framed prints on the coloured walls, for it was before the days of the plenitude of photography. The furniture was all of plain deal, stained dark brown and cocoa-nut matting on the floor.

To the south of this building, at the rear of the courtyard, was an annexe formerly used as workshops. The lowest level became the refectory where the nuns took their meals in 'a sort of semi-underground shed… It was as plain as plain could be, with brick walls and floor and trestle tables.' The upper workshop served as a dormitory, split into four cubicles, where Sister Kate slept. The lower workshop was converted into the oratory with a projecting dormer window, topped by a cross, added to the exterior. Inside it was 'Long and narrow, with dark wooden desks on each side for the Sisters and a sort of parc, shut off with wooden rails for the orphans.'[32]

The orphanage had been established in Brighton by Neale's younger sister Elizabeth. In April 1857 she was invited to set up her own community of Sisters in Wapping (subsequently Holy Cross, Hayward's Heath) and Neale agreed to integrate the orphans into St Margaret's. He rented a

Figure 14 *In 1858 the Sisters moved into no. 1 Church Lane, now Spires Hairdressing. The courtyard seen here is that illustrated in fig 3 with the oratory in the weatherboarded building at the rear. The Sisters also took over neighbouring properties as their numbers grew.*

house for them on the London Road until No. 77 High Street became available, next to Sackville College. By 1860 the 'blue-frocked, white-capped, rosy little crew' of thirteen had increased to twenty five with their accommodation now extending to the whole of the High Street terrace from Nos. 73-77, connected across the street front by a wooden cloister and linked at the rear via the annexe to the buildings on Church Lane.[33] This complex came to be known as St Margaret's Home. In the entrance courtyard stood a cross, carved from Devonshire marble, in memory of Sister Amy. Designed by Bodley, it was unveiled on 13 September 1858.[34] When the nuns moved they took it with them and the cross still stands in the quadrangle of the Old Convent on Moat Road.

With a secure abode the work of the Sisterhood was able to expand rapidly. As well as going out to nurse patients in their own homes, which they continued to do extensively and at increasing distances, the Sisters also cared for people in East Grinstead. This included both residents and people who came to their door seeking help. Sick callers were directed to the Ship Inn where their board and lodging was paid for by St Margaret's. At first the accommodation there was of such a poor standard that Mother Ann was forced to

Figure 15 *The tiny oratory of St Margaret's Home was converted from a tanning workshop. Note how everyone is veiled; the orphan girls and novices wear white, the St Agnes pupils wear blue and the Sisters wear black.*

threaten the withdrawal of their custom unless the landlord made improvements and stopped putting unrelated men, women and children in the same room. The meticulous diaries kept by the Sisters reveal that cases of terminal cancer were among those treated in this way.

Education also quickly became a core activity. St Agnes' School opened for the daughters of professional men in May 1862 and such was the gap this filled for girls' education that by the end of the year it was occupying two houses on Moat Road. A pre-fabricated school room, made of corrugated iron, was subsequently erected

Figure 16 *The orphanage occupied a terrace of three Victorian houses along East Grinstead High Street. These were linked at street level by a wooden cloister.*

behind the properties on Church Lane where it remains to this day. Additional provision was made for evening classes both on site and in local public houses. At the Ship Inn Sister Isabel taught West Indian and Irish immigrants alongside the regular lodgers. By Ash Wednesday 1858 she had nineteen people for instruction at The Ship and also gave classes at Mrs Pobgee's Ale House at Ashurst Wood (now the Rose and Crown).

When construction began on the railway extension to Tunbridge Wells, Neale immediately sent a Sister on to the line to

Figure 17 *The community took their meals in the refectory at the rear of the courtyard beneath the oratory. This contemporary watercolour shows a simple space with textual decoration praising God.*

read to the men every day at dinner time from midday to 1pm. The work done by railway navvies was crucial to the modernisation of Victorian Britain yet they were one of the most marginalised groups in society. Heavy drinking was normal among navvies and death from alcohol poisoning was common. Reaching out to them with the opportunity for betterment proved very welcome and twenty men signed up to attend the night school run in St Margaret's refectory four times a week.

During the exceptionally cold winter of 1859-60, Neale started a soup kitchen at St Margaret's. Operating from the Dorset Arms it was able to help 162 local families every week and served a total of 59 gallons of soup. Alongside this the Sisters gave out coal to keep the meagre fires of poor locals burning. All this charitable work cost money and in a letter of 14 September 1861 Neale informed his friend Benjamin Webb that '...S Margaret's will cost nearly £3,000 this year.'[35] After the furore of the Lewes Riots had died down donations picked up again but the Sisters also raised funds by their own endeavours. In autumn 1859 they took delivery of a printing press and a man came from London to teach them how to use it. Sister Kate was one of those given lessons and recalled how 'Mr Wagner of S. Paul's Brighton sent us an order for 200 copies of an advent hymn at 5s a hundred, so we worked hard setting up the type and printing them off. We felt so proud!'[36] By 1859 they had also begun taking the commissions for ecclesiastical embroidery which will be discussed further in chapter four.

With so much variety of useful work there was a sense of achievement within the Sisterhood that helped feed the expanding mission beyond East Grinstead. Sister Kate recalled in 1903 how half a century earlier:

> Young ladies never dreamed of the wider possibilities open to them now; there were no Ladies' Settlements, no Lady Nurses, no Girton, Newnham, St Margaret's. They gardened, they sketched, rode, went to archery meetings and were just beginning to visit their poor and teach in the Sunday school. The emancipation of women had not yet then arrived...[37]

What she found upon joining St Margaret's was a feeling of shared purpose among a community of women who all wanted to contribute more than society expected of them; 'There was always such a happy, homey truthfulness about those early days of

St Margaret's. Nothing seemed too great to attempt, nothing seemed too remote to hope for. We would have dared and done anything.'[38] By November 1861, St Margaret's was the country's second largest Sisterhood behind Clewer and it was becoming increasingly clear that a purpose-built convent was required.

Figure 18 *The first generation of Sisters photographed in 1895 - front row, left to right shows Sr Ermenild (John Mason Neale's daughter), Sr Frances, Sr Lucy, Mother Alice, Sr Isa (professed respectively in 1868, 1864, 1856, 1863) and back row second from right, Sr Gertrude (professed 1866).*

Figure 19 *The quadrangle looking west.*

Chapter 2
A Purpose-built Convent

In 1863 the Bishop of Chichester formally withdrew his inhibition of Neale. After a battle of sixteen years Neale had finally gained tacit approval though he was never informed of why the ban was lifted: 'I have neither withdrawn a single word, nor altered a single practice (except in a few instances by way of going further.)'[39] Soon after this a new Vicar, the Rev I Peat, arrived in East Grinstead proving friendly both to Neale and the Sisterhood. Local attitudes were so altered that a decade after its inception plans could begin to build St Margaret's a proper convent. The word had not been used before in case it stirred up trouble but its meaning, from the Latin 'conventus', to convene or come together, summed up the

Figure 20 *An early aerial view of the convent.*

spirit and the necessity of bringing all the elements of the expanding community onto one site. In April 1864 Neale went to inspect a plot of land with two friends, the architect George Edmund Street and the Rev. John Comper, sponsor of St Margaret's first daughter house at Aberdeen. By summer the land was purchased and Neale wrote of it to his good friend Joseph Haskoll, rector of East Bark with Wragby in Lincolnshire: 'You remember the London road. Well, if you go down that about three-quarters of a mile, it will then lie a third of a mile to your right. The view to the north is very lovely, over the Surrey hills. The field is ten acres.'[40]

As a client, Neale was unusually well-informed but he had also secured the services, for free, of an architect whose religious views mirrored his own and for whom designing Gothic buildings was an act of faith. With such a combination St Margaret's Convent was always going to be something special. This chapter explores how its design fits into the wider Gothic Revival and the career of its designer G E Street.

The Gothic Revival and the Cambridge Camden Society

From the 1830s British architects fell prey to what has become known as the 'dilemma of style'. Industrialisation had transformed society and introduced new building materials, in particular iron, for which there was no stylistic precedent. Knowledge of foreign architecture was also increasing and this caused real anxiety about the best way to express contemporary ideals and concerns through building. Classical architecture, based on Greek and Roman models, defined the Georgian era and continued to be used throughout the nineteenth century. However, this was an imported style and many young architects wanted both a break with the recent past and a more obviously British prototype.

Among the styles competing to represent Victorian values, Gothic became one of the most influential. It had never entirely gone away as an appropriate style for church building but took on greater potency thanks to the Oxford Movement and the ardent promotion of Augustus Welby Northmore Pugin (1812-52), the man who gave the Houses of Parliament their Gothic ornament. He brilliantly capitalised on a growing interest in Britain's

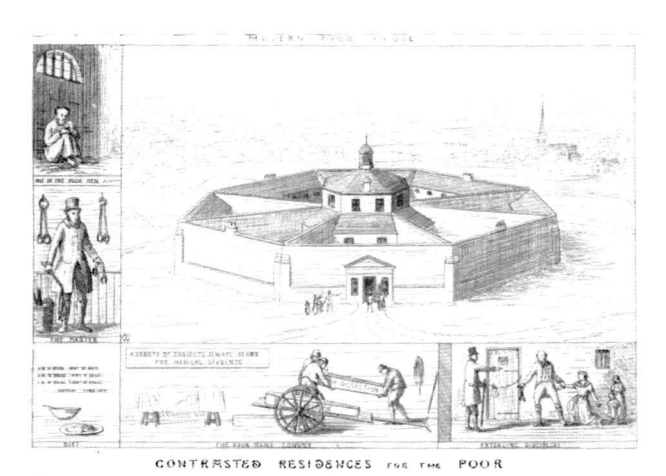

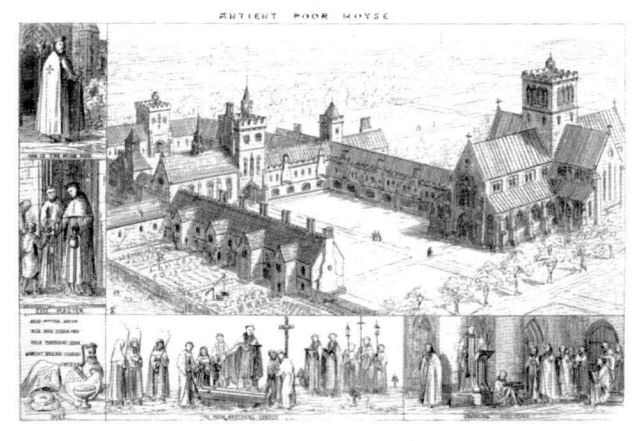

Figure 21 *AWN Pugin used his book* Contrasts *to promote the architecture and social structures of the pre-Reformation period. In this illustration he set the treatment of medieval paupers in a monastic setting against the degradation of the Victorian workhouse.*

medieval past and, following his conversion to Roman Catholicism in 1834, stridently set forth his argument for the purity of Gothic. Pugin's desire was to see a national return to Catholicism as well as its finest period of artistic expression. In his view the Reformation had cut the crucial tie between religion and art. The Renaissance had then finished the job by reviving classical, pagan forms of architecture. Pugin hated the buildings of his century and made his disgust clear in his book of *Contrasts* published in 1836 and again in 1841. Its subtitle was 'a Parallel between the Noble Edifices of the Fourteenth and Fifteenth Centuries, and Similar Buildings of the Present Day: Shewing the Present Decay of Taste…' This was not confined to church architecture. He also compared relief of the poor in monasteries and almshouses with the modern day workhouse, in which the master gave out lashes from his whip instead of alms, the wretched inhabitants were fed on bread and gruel and their spiritual afterlife was given so little thought that their bodies were given up for dissection. In two drawings on a single page he summed up the moral bankruptcy he saw around him. Continuing this highly effective propaganda he portrayed two contrasted towns in 1440 and 1840 with the rise of unadulterated capitalism writ large in the Victorian skyline of chimneys where before had been spires raised to the glory of God.

Figure 22 *Neale bemoaned the disregard for the altar shown by low church Evangelicals. This pair of illustrations from Augustine David Crake's book* Deformation and Reformation *(c1870) uses Pugin's polemical technique to contrast an untidy table under a plain window with the highly decorated Anglo-Catholic sanctuary.*

The key feature of the emerging Gothic Revival was the pointed arch; the style itself was often referred to as 'Pointed'. In his 1841 book *The True Principles of Pointed or Christian Architecture*, Pugin set out to make it unassailable: 'we can never successfully deviate one tittle from the spirit and principles of pointed architecture. We must rest content to follow not to lead.'[41] This dogmatic approach was adopted by the Cambridge Camden Society which spread Pugin's message within the Church of England in a way that he, as a Catholic convert, could not.

Romanticism provided the cultural backdrop to this renewed interest in Gothic architecture. A literary and philosophical movement, it was also seeking inspiration from the past. No writer captured the chivalric ideal so well as Sir Walter Scott whose pen created the Victorian image of the middle ages subsequently handed down to us through the era's artistic output. Though the Oxford Tractarians sought to revive church doctrine from the same period they had little interest in aesthetics. John Mason Neale, whose literary works included poetry and fiction, was far more susceptible to the romance of medievalism which he believed could be used to engage the hearts and minds of ordinary people. For him it was evident that 'the very structure and furnishing of church buildings, together with appropriate ritual within services, could lead a soul to more profound worship.'[42] It was with the goal of restoring beauty to the church as a means of encouraging attendance that he and his fellow undergraduates Edward Boyce and Benjamin Webb, created the Cambridge Camden Society (CCS) in 1839.

All members of the CCS were tasked with visiting or 'taking' churches, around Cambridge every week. This not only provided them with evidence of the dereliction against which they fought but also helped add to their store of knowledge about how Gothic masons worked and designed. A member visiting the village of Haslingfield found that 'The church has suffered considerably from damp and neglect; the state of the floor at the west end of the north aisle is such as would certainly not be permitted in any gentleman's stable, nor, voluntarily, in the meanest cottage.'[43] Neale himself saw repeated proof that reverence for church buildings was at an all time low. On his first Sunday as a parish priest in Crawley, 'in the middle of the service...the Church warden, wanting to open the east window, got up on the Altar!'[44] Understanding was key to appreciation and since there appeared to be little of either in the wider church community the CCS developed their fact-finding into a rigorous

Figure 23 *The richly ornamented interior of William Butterfield's All Saint's Margaret Street in Westminster marked a turning point in the development of Victorian Gothic.*

new science of church architecture which they called 'ecclesiology'. Members were given a pro forma to complete when taking churches and as membership began to spread beyond Cambridge University the collection of data also widened. The Society's reforming agenda was also pushed through the pages of its monthly publication which first appeared in November 1841 under the title, suggested by Neale, of *The Ecclesiologist*.

From a mere thirty-eight members in 1839 the CCS grew rapidly, reaching 300 members within two years. By 1843, when Neale stepped down as Chairman, Boyce recorded that membership included '2 Archbishops, 16 Bishops, 31 Peers and MPs, 7 Deans and Chancellors of Dioceses, 21 Archdeacons and Rural Deans, 16 Architects, and over 700 ordinary members.'[45] Among the architects was George (later Sir George) Gilbert Scott. He became aware of the CCS having read an article by Benjamin Webb sometime around 1842. This led him to seek a meeting at which ' Mr. Webb took advantage of the occasion to lecture me on church architecture in general, on the necessity of chancels &c. &c. I at once saw that he was right and became a reader of the "Ecclesiologist"'.[46] Scott simultaneously read Pugin's articles in the *Dublin Review* which, as he recalled in his autobiography, 'excited me

Figure 24 *In c1847 Neale commissioned Butterfield to redesign the chapel of Sackville College, East Grinstead. The insertion of a rood screen with cross was highly controversial at the time.*

almost to a fury, and I suddenly found myself like a person awakened from a long feverish dream, which had rendered him unconscious of what was going on about him.'[47] From that point onward Scott's approach to church building changed as he set out to formulate a version of 'Middle Pointed', or late thirteenth century Decorated English Gothic, adapted for modern worship using modern materials and building technology. It made him extremely successful and many of the 700 or more commissions he undertook during his career were for churches in this manner. Yet, the seeds of a more radical phase of Victorian Gothic were already growing in the fertile soil of his office where the next generation of Goths, George Edmund Street, William White and George Frederick Bodley, were in training.

Around mid-century a shift occurred away from the concept of a Gothic 'revival' that simply re-used medieval forms towards a belief that Gothic should be 'developed' to suit contemporary needs. All the architects employed by John Mason Neale worked in this so called 'High Victorian' style, indeed they were the leaders of this new *avant garde* and all of them were members of the CCS which, in 1846, moved to London and became the Ecclesiological Society. The first complete expression of High Victorian Gothic was the London church of All Saint's, Margaret Street designed in 1849-50 by William Butterfield (1814-1900). In the first half of the 1840s Butterfield had virtually assumed the role of in-house designer for the Ecclesiologists meaning Neale knew him well. The Society was run by, and effectively represented the theological and architectural views of, its executive committee. Neale remained joint secretary until 1849 and was a frequent contributor to *The Ecclesiologist* which was also edited by the committee; though reports of church building projects, visits and restorations were anonymous, an annotated copy of the first edition shows that he wrote forty seven of the 157 articles.[48] This made Neale an extremely influential figure and one whose patronage counted. Soon after his move to East Grinstead in 1846 Neale commissioned Butterfield to restore the chapel at Sackville College according to their shared Gothic tastes. Despite being a small job it mattered as a demonstration of what 'good' ecclesiology should look like. As time moved on this increasingly meant stripping Gothic back to its essentials and reinvigorating it by learning from periods other than the Middle Pointed and taking inspiration from foreign examples. It was in this High Gothic idiom that the Convent of St Margaret's would be built.

G E Street and the design for St Margaret's

George Edmund Street was born on 20 June 1824 at Woodford in Essex, the second son of Thomas Street, a solicitor. His preferred career choice would have been to enter the church as a priest but, after his father's death in 1840, there was insufficient money to fund the university education this required. Street's artistic talent had, however, already become apparent. In autumn 1839, aged fifteen, Street joined his elder brother Thomas on a sketching trip around churches and old houses near their mother's home in Crediton, Devon. They made a similar trip into North Devon the following year after which Street was sent to have drawing lessons with an artist Mr Haseler, an uncle by marriage, who lived at Taunton. Another family connection secured him a place as pupil in the office of Winchester architect Owen Browne Carter from 1841. After three years working for provincial clients he was desperate to find a more stimulating practice. Taking himself to London he was accepted as an assistant in the office of George Gilbert Scott then working on plans for the Lutheran church of St Nicholas in Hamburg. Throughout this time Street spent his holidays 'ecclesiologising' or church hunting with his brother. He joined the CCS in 1845.

Figure 25 *This portrait of George Edmund Street was published in an 1877 series called* Men of Mark. *The accompanying text mentioned St Margaret's convent as nearing completion.*

Architectural historian Michael Hall has described Scott's office as 'a liberating environment, both artistically and intellectually...a nursery for outstanding talent...'[49] Scott left his craftsmen, pupils and assistants to fill in much of the detail of his designs but, just as important as these opportunities for self-expression, were the friendships Street made. William White joined as an assistant in 1845 and George Frederick Bodley as a pupil in 1846. Forming a discernible coterie within the office, the three of them all rejected Scott's architectural approach when setting up on their own, instead taking Gothic forward in new directions. Street got his first independent commission for a church at Biscovey in Cornwall in 1846 and had sufficient work to establish his own practice by 1849. He moved to Wantage, then in Berkshire, upon his appointment as Oxford diocesan architect in 1850. Two years later, and following his marriage to Mariquita Proctor, Street moved to Oxford itself. With a growing national reputation he returned to London in 1856 where he stayed for the rest of his life.

Although George Gilbert Scott embraced Gothic he was not a Tractarian. Street, White and Bodley were. This proved to be a crucial difference because as the High Church Anglican movement became embattled around 1850 its exponents looked to embody their programme of change in architectural form and allied themselves with the emerging High Victorian Gothic style. In 1855 Neale went to Bodley to design the first oratory for his Sisterhood at No. 8 Church Lane, East Grinstead employing him again three years later to convert a number of adjoining buildings into St Margaret's Home (see p33). During this period Neale also sought designs from Street so the convent on Moat Road was by no means the first time they had worked together.

In George Edmund Street, Neale found something of a kindred spirit. Neale's introduction to the translation of William Durand's 1285 *Rationale Divinorum Officiorum*, published by the Ecclesiological Society in 1843 as *The Symbolism of Churches and Church Ornament,* set a high standard for church architects to meet. He imagined the fourteenth century flowering of ecclesiastical architecture to have been the work of religious orders, churches and cathedrals springing from the minds of devout men with no concern for money. Such a romantic vision made Neale regret the nineteenth century professionalisation of architecture and yet in Street he found someone who truly embodied his belief, as summarised by biographer Michael Chandler, that 'a Catholic architect must have a Catholic heart and live sacrificially.'[50] In 1848 Street had been involved in a scheme, based on the idea of a medieval guild of architects, to create a society or college where students would be instructed in religious art whilst living under religious ordinances, in accord with the 'lofty character of their work'.[51] Though this came to nothing Street maintained a deep and indivisible connection between his own religious beliefs and his work as an architect. When he moved to Wantage to work there for the Rev William John Butler, founder of the Sisterhood of St Mary the Virgin, he attended daily service and joined the choir. After relocating to London he became one of the most active lay members in the congregation of All Saints, Margaret Street and from 1867-71 served as a churchwarden there.

Street's son states that by 1853 his father 'had long been on terms of intimacy with Mr. Neale'.[52] This was certainly through the Ecclesiological Society where Street was in the habit of giving lectures and for whom he had made designs for 'every possible kind of church fitting and furniture', some of which were made up for display at the Great Exhibition of 1851.[53] On 24 November 1854 Street made designs for the fitting up of a 'Lych Room' at Sackville College, probably meant for the reception of deceased residents awaiting their funeral.

Wooden panelling was to be inserted into a small existing room with iron-hinged shutters added to the windows. At the same time, Street provided Neale with designs for an elaborate gabled ironwork hearse frame that enclosed a wooden funeral bier.[54] Neither design was executed, nor do they seem to relate to preparations for beginning the Sisterhood. The following year, however, as support for his proposed nursing order grew, Neale confidently asked his friend Street to make drawings for an entirely new building.

Neale's enthusiasm for new projects was boundless and the following letter from Street, written on 22 February 1855 when St Margaret's was barely in existence, shows how he was already thinking ahead in a wholly innovative way:

My dear Neale,

I was in town for a few days when your letter arrived, so that I was unable to do what you asked immediately.

I have, however, now made a plan which will, I hope, be sent to you in the course of to-morrow.

I have made a very simple and unornamented cottage. On the ground floor is a sick room for men, a small doctor's room, and a kitchen; and on the first floor a sick room for women, linen closet, a sleeping room for a Sister of Mercy, and another small room which might be used either as a second room for her, or as an oratory...

It is difficult to make a design without any reference to a particular locality. At least I always find it to be so; and it is probable that such a plan as I have made might in nine cases out of ten be unavailable. I shall, however, be very glad if I have done anything to help your work, and I think the scheme of your Sisterhood very admirable; if thoroughly carried out, it will tell both on the people and on their priest, wherever it is brought to work.

Believe me always, yours very faithfully,

George Edmund Street[55]

WEST ELEVATION

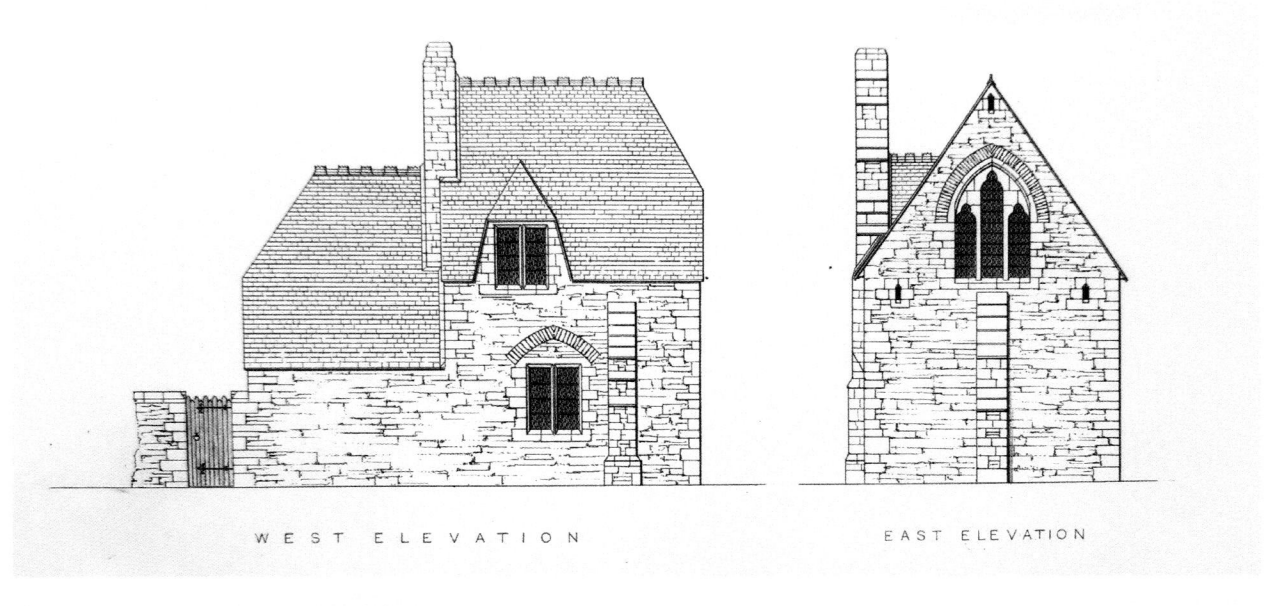

EAST ELEVATION

SOUTH ELEVATION

Figure 26 *Designs for a 'Village Hospital' by G E Street, published by the Cambridge Camden Society in their* Instrumenta Ecclesiastica, *vol. 2, 1856*

It was only four months earlier, in November 1854, that Spencer Thomson MD had mooted the concept of a cottage hospital in a letter to the *British Medical Journal*. The doctor from Burton-on-Trent had proposed that 'the evil of the sick poor being treated in their over-crowded dwellings… might be alleviated by having…a sort of "Cottage Hospital", that is a small house…devoted to the reception of the sick…' Historians date the opening of the first actual cottage hospital to 1860 when Dr Napper began treating poor people for free in a converted cottage at Cranleigh in Surrey.[56] Though the scheme discussed by Neale and Street proved premature the designs were published by the Ecclesiological Society in their 1856 book *Instrumenta Ecclesiastica*. Reproduced at fig 26 these are arguably the first ever drawings for a purpose-built cottage hospital and in their simple elevations, handled in Street's version of domestic Gothic, they show a clear resemblance to the later convent at East Grinstead.

It was to be another decade before conditions were right to begin St Margaret's Convent. With John Mason Neale's long study of, and deeply-held views on, Gothic architecture the design of the convent held immense importance as a propaganda exercise. As Anson put it, in the mid-1860s 'there was no conventual establishment anywhere in Britain planned on such a magnificent scale and with such apparent indifference to cost.' Neale had been waiting his whole life for this opportunity and 'If St Margaret's Convent did not convince people that England's Church was catholic, nothing would!'[57] His obituary in *The Ecclesiologist* stated that in the buildings 'from Mr Street's designs, but under his own personal supervision, he turned his great practical knowledge of Pointed architecture to good account.'[58] The project was personal for Street too and, in a paper read to the Ecclesiological Society in 1953 H S Goodhart-Rendel called it his 'own darling work in secular architecture.'[59] A visitor to the celebrations for laying the foundation stone in 1865 noted that 'The architect Mr Street, gives his design and work gratis, as a labour of love. Considering the demand upon his time in all directions, this is no small gift.'[60] In 1864, when he made the first designs, Street was also building churches in Constantinople [Istanbul] and Genoa and stated that 'As to my works in England, they are only too numerous and I really have great difficulty in getting them all done. I must not grumble at being so prosperous. I suppose, really, that now there is no other architect among the Gothic men, save Scott, who has anything like as much as I have to do.'[61]

Figure 27 *Hackenden quarry provided stone for the convent. It survives in an area of wasteland next to the railway line into East Grinstead.*

Street was that rare architect who could visit a site and almost immediately conceive of the building he would erect there. The field off Moat Road in East Grinstead not only had fine views but also a nearby source of materials which Street no doubt investigated on his preliminary visit with Neale. In August 1864 the latter could report that 'We have also bought a quarry about three hundred yards off; so we shall have no expense in cartage. That stone will do for the walls: plain mullions we can get from a quarry at Ashurst Wood: it is not a pretty coloured sandstone – tawny red – but good. Our quarry is white, with a few iron stains.'[62] It made economic sense to purchase the quarry at Hackenden but there was also an important philosophical point to using local materials. From his extensive studies of old buildings Street concluded that vernacular styles were almost always the result of using the materials closest to hand, 'the best art being found near the best quarries.'[63] The expanding Victorian rail network allowed for transport of brick and slate to anywhere in the country but, reacting against this mass-manufactured uniformity, Street's call for a return to the vernacular became a key tenet of the Arts and Crafts Movement as espoused by his assistants Philip Webb (1831-1915), William Morris (1834-96), Edmund and John Dando Sedding (1836-68, 1838-91) and Richard Norman Shaw (1831-1912).

As for the design of the convent, Street already had experience of several similar projects. From 1855 he had built the convent of St Mary the Virgin at Wantage for his first key patron William Butler, later Dean of Lincoln. This consisted of courtyards separated by a refectory and from 1858-61 Street added the Chapel of St Mary Magdalene. In his role as Oxford diocesan architect, Street enjoyed the patronage and friendship of Bishop Samuel Wilberforce who commissioned him to design the Theological College at Cuddesdon in 1852 (fig 28). This building is generally considered to mark the beginning of his mature career. In his *Dictionary of National Biography* (DNB) entry for Street, David Brownlee notes that at Cuddesdon 'the growing energy of his style seems to emerge almost unbidden from the local vernacular.' For architectural historian Henry-Russell Hitchcock 'the picturesqueness of the design derives from the 'sternest utility'...There is little detail and everything is very 'real' ie., masonlike...' Street's son claimed this was the result of lack of funds 'but the absence of enrichment is not noticed, nor is its want felt, because of the admirable proportions and grouping of the whole building.' Significantly A E Street considered that the design for St Margaret's 'was on somewhat the same lines as that for Cuddesdon College, but perhaps a little more mannered than it, and somewhat ultra-monastic and severe in character.'[64] The first historian of the Gothic Revival, Charles Eastlake, drew the same parallel as early as 1872 when he stated that 'Nothing can possibly be simpler than...[Street's] works at Cuddesdon and East Grinstead...They have literally no architectural character beyond what may be secured by stout masonry, a steep roof and a few dormer windows.' Despite this 'there is genuine *cachet* on each design which is impossible to mistake. They are the production of an artist hand.'[65]

A third precedent was the Collegiate Institute commissioned in 1854 by Rev John W Hewett at Bloxham near Banbury. Street's most ambitious scheme to date, it was only partially built but a drawing survives in the archives of Bloxham

Figure 28 *Street's design for Cuddesdon College was published in* The Building News *of 6 August 1875. Like St Margaret's it featured asymmetrical elevations with multiple gables.*

School (fig 29). Hitchcock's article on Street during the 1850s included this description of a perspective lithograph of Bloxham:

> There were two courtyards, the larger enclosed by school rooms, chapel, refectory, etc. the smaller surrounding (of all things) a graveyard. Kitchens etc., were given a separate block south of the refectory. The materials were to be of local stone…

….It is in [Street's] Berkshire parsonage and Cuddesdon manner – a variant on English Geometrical Decorated…Dormers of various designs, steep roofs at difference levels, diverse methods of fenestration, bold use of projecting gables and positioning of slab-like chimneys, emphatic buttresses and strings give much plastic richness without distracting from strong massing of volumes…[66]

Figure 29 *All Saints School, Bloxham was designed around a quadrangle with cloistered walks and roofs punctuated by dormers. An ambitious scheme, it was only partially executed to Street's proposals.*

Stylistically St Margaret's has always been included in this group from the 1850s. This has previously been explained by Philip Webb's reference, in the first DNB entry for Street, to plans made for Neale at this time. We now know these drawings related to a cottage hospital not the convent. Though St Margaret's was designed a decade later it nonetheless shows clear parallels with these earlier projects and Neale's preference for Puginian English Pointed may partially explain this. His advocacy of this style through *The Ecclesiologist* was well known making Hitchcock's assessment of the convent all the more pertinent: '...the whole effect is such as Pugin should have approved – quiet, easy and yet with a solidity of simple craftsmanship in stone that Pugin himself had rarely been able to achieve.'[67]

The most fascinating thing about the convent design, however, is the way in which it gradually moved away from this mid-century Puginian iteration. Street's later commissions show greater influence from his travels through France, Italy, Germany and Spain, adding Continental references into a 'developed' Gothic of his own making. At East Grinstead inspiration for the final form came from Flemish and North German models.

Figure 30 *The saddleback tower is not an English feature but one used by Street and Bodley to reference the Gothic of Northern Europe. This travel drawing appeared in Street's 1855 book* Brick and Marble in the Middle Ages: Notes of Tours in the North of Italy.

Indeed the debt to Low Countries architecture is an important part of the overall mix, most visible in the tower's saddleback roof design. With this, Street combined fourteenth century and Tudor details as well as some direct borrowings, for instance the door into the chapel at the end of the cloister with dog-tooth frame, which recalls one at St Augustine's, Bristol. All these influences were skilfully melded together to create a whole that is of its own time.

Figure 31 G F Bodley's church of All Saints at Selsey, Gloucestershire featured an early use of the Continental saddleback tower in 1861-2.

Laying the Foundation Stone

The 20 July 1865 dawned as a day of great excitement in East Grinstead. John Mason Neale had gone to considerable effort to turn the laying of St Margaret's foundation stone into a grand occasion. Clergymen from across the country were invited to stay in the school dormitories of St Agnes' which were vacant for the summer holidays, while hundreds more people arrived on the day itself. A special train was laid on from Victoria which connected to the London Bridge service at Three Bridges. Tickets for the celebratory luncheon could be bought at a cost of 3s 6d from shops in East Grinstead, London and Brighton. It was noteworthy that the greater part of people attending came from the latter two places whereas members of the local gentry stayed away. Judging by the number of press accounts a good number of journalists also made the day trip. These commentators tell us what an 'exquisitely fine' day it was, with brilliant sunshine and a 'slight refreshing breeze...'[68] From noon, two hundred or so people began to amass at Sackville College where the three or four resident peacocks 'watched with ludicrous gravity, the procession as it formed in the quadrangle...'[69]

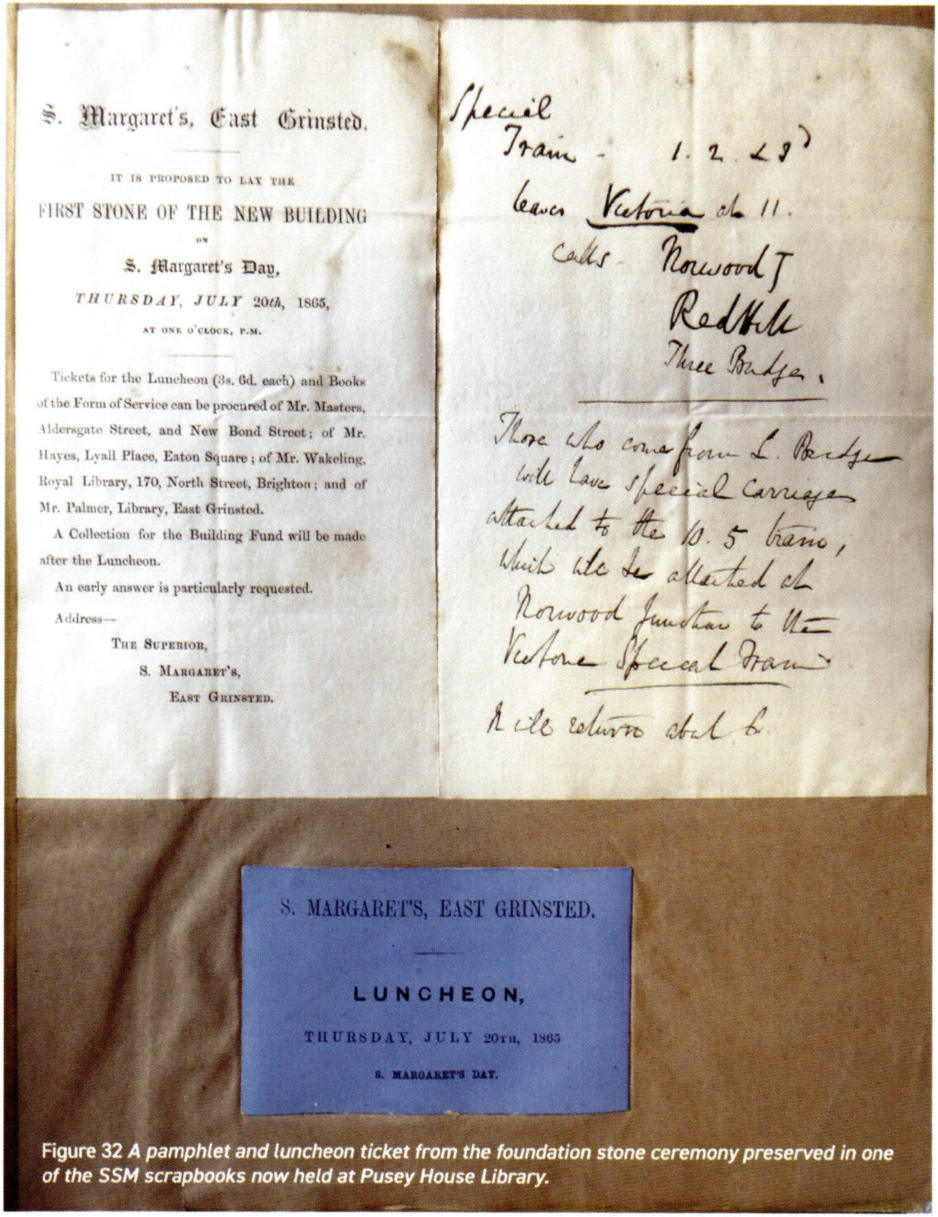

S. Margaret's, East Grinsted.

IT IS PROPOSED TO LAY THE

FIRST STONE OF THE NEW BUILDING

ON

S. Margaret's Day,

THURSDAY, JULY 20th, 1865,

AT ONE O'CLOCK, P.M.

Tickets for the Luncheon (3s. 6d. each) and Books of the Form of Service can be procured of Mr. Masters, Aldersgate Street, and New Bond Street; of Mr. Hayes, Lyall Place, Eaton Square; of Mr. Wakeling, Royal Library, 170, North Street, Brighton; and of Mr. Palmer, Library, East Grinsted.

A Collection for the Building Fund will be made after the Luncheon.

An early answer is particularly requested.

Address—

THE SUPERIOR,
S. MARGARET'S,
EAST GRINSTED.

Special Train — 1. 2. 23?
leaves Victoria at 11.
Calls — Norwood J
Redhill
Three Bridges.

Those who come from L. Bridge will have special carriage attached to the 10.5 train, which will be attached at Norwood Junction to the Victoria Special Train.

It will return about 6.

S. MARGARET'S, EAST GRINSTED.

LUNCHEON,

THURSDAY, JULY 20TH, 1865

S. MARGARET'S DAY.

Figure 32 *A pamphlet and luncheon ticket from the foundation stone ceremony preserved in one of the SSM scrapbooks now held at Pusey House Library.*

Figure 33 *The annual St Margaret's Day procession, begun in 1865, happened for more than a century. This photograph of the orphans processing behind Sr Margaret was taken in 1923.*

Taking account of the previous rioting against him, Neale planned his procession route across open fields avoiding the town centre and any potential trouble. Sentiment in East Grinstead had undergone such change, however, that he found '...the townspeople were so *horribly* disappointed...we have engaged to go through the town [instead]. It shews how completely we can trust them, that I have not the LEAST anxiety in letting some thirty girls and the Sisters...do this.'[70] Processing behind a crimson and blue banner embroidered to the designs of Edmund and John Sedding, the girls of St Margaret's orphanage led the way. They were followed by the Sisters of St Margaret, with Novices in white veils behind them. Next came the Sisters visiting from other communities, then the Mother Superior with Francis Barchard and four choirs drawn from Stoke Newington, Brighton, Soho and Clapham. Members of the clergy brought up the rear. At the very end walked Neale with two friends from the Eastern Church, Rev Eugene Popoff, Chaplain of the Russian Embassy, and the Greek Orthodox Archimandrite of Liverpool, the most Rev Constantine Stratuli. To the sound of chanting this emphatically High Church procession wound its way through East Grinstead, Neale declaring that it was 'nearly a quarter of a mile long, and so *very* beautiful.'[71]

Figure 34 *Francis Barchard was a wealthy lawyer who became a trustee of SSM and laid the foundation stones of many of the convent buildings. A keen amateur photographer, Barchard's Family Album in the V&A Museum includes several pictures relating to SSM. The photograph at Figure 35, taken in 1915, shows the location of the original foundation stone laid by Barchard between the two windows on the corner of the oratory.*

It took about an hour for everyone to arrive at Moat Road for the ceremonial laying of the foundation stone. Despite Mother Ann going in person to invite the Bishop of Chichester he had refused to attend. At short notice Francis Barchard agreed to take his place. Barchard was a barrister who lived at Horsted Place near Uckfield. This grand country house was built by his father, also called Francis, who had inherited a large fortune from his godfather's Wandsworth dyeing business. Horsted Place was in the same parish as Rotherfield so Barchard and his wife Aretina were already friendly with Mother Ann. They were keen supporters of the Oxford Movement and the Society of St Margaret in particular. Francis Barchard became a trustee in 1864 and was known as Warden of the Community after Neale's death. As well as laying the convent's foundation stone in 1865, Barchard also laid the foundation stone of the chapel in 1879, repeating this role for the guest house ten years later.

The location of the foundation stone is unmarked but was in the corner of the original oratory. This space would later become the orphanage sewing room and is now in house No. 13 within the quadrangle (fig 35). The following description from *The Guardian* was based on a birds-eye view (fig 36) produced to help guests visualise the proposed buildings designed for forty nuns and 120 girls in the orphanage and school.

> It will consist of a quadrangle of considerable extent. The principal entrance will be on the western side, which will be occupied with the apartments of the Assistant Superior and the serving Sisters. On the north will be the orphans' school, and apartments for strangers. On the east side will be lodged the Mother Superior and the Sisters, each having a private room or cell, which will not be occupied when she is away on duty. Beyond this a parallel wing will be built for St Agnes' School. The south side will contain the chapel and hall, to the south of which will be the burial-garth, and still more southerly an infirmary. The kitchens and offices will also be in a separate building on the south side. Returning to the quadrangle, it will contain a cloister, running round its four sides; and there will be a large and handsome cross in the centre [that dedicated to Sister Amy and relocated from Church Lane]. At the north-west angle there will be an oratory, the corner stone of which was selected for the ceremony…if a judgement may be formed from

> a lithographed perspective which has been prepared from the architect's plans, it may be confidently anticipated that the buildings will form a most effective and artistic group. At present, however, the funds which have been collected will only permit the execution of the north and west sides of the quadrangle.[72]

Aware that financing would be an issue, Street and Neale had planned for a phased construction schedule.

Most of the guests invited to the foundation stone ceremony donated to the building fund with some 360 people staying on for the luncheon prepared by Mr W Head of the Crown Inn, East Grinstead and served in a marquee. As was typical of Victorian events such as this, the meal was followed by numerous votes of thanks. Also typical was the fact that these were all given by men despite the project being intended almost exclusively for women. The *Sussex Express* actually noted that 'the majority of those present were ladies, the quaint dresses of the Sisterhood mingling strangely with the gay dresses of some of their less devoted sex.'[73] Once the celebration was over the real hard work of building and fundraising commenced.

Figure 36 *This 1865 view was produced to assist fundraising but appears never to have been published. Key features, including the chapel tower, kitchen and range of Sister's cells (which here closely resemble the quad interior at Bloxham) underwent substantial change in later designs.*

Figure 37 *Details of the stone pulpit in the refectory from an original drawing by Street.*

Chapter 3
The Progress of Works

Phase One: 1865-74

As construction got underway Neale was a frequent visitor to the site. On 19 September 1865 he wrote to his friend Haskoll that 'The new Convent gets on gloriously. The scaffolding is setting up. To-day the 'crabs' [ie. scaffolders] begin to work.'[74] Neale enjoyed a good relationship with the workmen and, concerned that they should appreciate what they were building and behave in a way that reflected well on the Sisterhood, he wrote a pamphlet addressed to them in 1866. In it he set out the reasons for the community's establishment and introduced its namesake Margaret of Antioch who was martyred aged eighteen on 20 July 1216, hence the date of St Margaret's Day. From this document we know that between thirty and forty workmen were employed: masons, carpenters, bricklayers, tram-men and quarry men, the latter extracting stone at Hackenden. All of them were outsiders so Neale asked them to consider the effect their arrival might have on a small country town. If they were of a kind to swear and drink this could be highly detrimental yet if the same men were 'honest, straightforward, obliging, they may do much good, even more than the money they spend in lodging, cooking, washing etc.' The potential economic benefit of a large workforce taking up residence over the course of a long construction project was clear but the Sisterhood was also 'thankful to God that from all we hear, we have reason to hope your coming here will be looked upon as having been a real blessing for East Grinstead.'[75]

This conclusion may have been, in part, due to the choice of contractor. The job went to John Fabian (1819-78), a master builder born in Portsea, Hampshire, who inherited the Brighton business of his uncle, also called John Fabian. By 1861 he had 128 men in his employ. His commissions at this time also show that he was a preferred contractor for Fr Henry Michell Wagner and his son Rev Arthur Douglas Wagner, both key clergy in the Oxford Movement on the south coast. St Paul's, Brighton was the first church funded by the Wagner family to open in 1848. In 1861-2 they built the mission chapel of St Mary the Virgin and St Mary Magdalene, Bread Street, as well as St Michael and All Angels, the most ritually advanced church in Sussex. George Frederick Bodley was architect of both these buildings; the contractor was John Fabian. Not only was there an obvious link here to Street and Neale but the Wagner connection extended to Mother Ann as well since the Brighton Sisterhood of which her sister Katherine was Superior, had also been founded by Arthur

Figure 38 *The church of St Michael and All Angels, Brighton soon after it was completed to the designs of G F Bodley in 1861. The contractor was John Fabian and the photographer was Francis Barchard.*

Douglas Wagner. Such a network helped ensure employment of a sympathetic builder.

Mr Fabian estimated that the first phase of work – to include the west range and gatehouse, north range, refectory and refectory cloister, kitchens and laundry – would cost £10,000. As with every building project there were unforeseen problems and in early January 1866 bad weather was the cause of one:

> We have had a most dreadful snowstorm, ushered in by thunder and lightning, and a tempest the whole day. More snow fell that day here than on any one day within living memory of man. The whole of the north side of our scaffold poles, though double braced, were torn out of the ground; and the east poles were so distressed that they will have to be taken down. This disaster will cost us £20. Providentially it happened at night.[76]

Not long afterwards, Neale's precarious health began to deteriorate. When his strength allowed he was pushed to the building site in his bath chair but after five months of suffering, 'with scarcely an interval of rallying, he passed away on the 6th of August [1866], at two in the morning, leaving behind him a reputation

Figure 39 *John Mason Neale was buried in St Swithun's churchyard in the shadow of St Margaret's Home.*

for unrivalled scholarship, for lyric grace, for unostentatious devotion and for gallant daring in the noblest of causes.'[77] Aged just forty-eight, his obituarist in *The Ecclesiologist* stated, with good reason, that 'He died, worn out...with incessant work...'[78]

Little more than a year after the celebrations to lay the foundation stone of St Margaret's, Neale's funeral produced another grand procession, the like of which, according to the *Church Times,* had not been 'seen in England (except perhaps at coronations) for three hundred years'.[79] Neale had planned every detail long before his death with services held in the oratory on Church Lane and Sackville College chapel before the church funeral and interment. 'Most of the shops were shut and many persons wore mourning. An immense crowd filled the streets, the Church and the Churchyard; and especially noticeable was a large number of navvies, who came to shew their gratitude to one who had taken great interest in them, and the workmen from the new convent, who gave up work on purpose to be present.'[80] For his final resting place Neale had chosen a plot in the south east corner of the churchyard directly opposite St Margaret's Home and 'it was indeed a touching sight to

Figure 40 *A photograph of Mother Alice taken from her obituary notice in 1902. She was in her mid-twenties when she joined SSM as one of the first Sisters.*

see the rows of [the orphans'] little faces at the upper window watching with childish curiosity the funeral of their more than father.' That Neale remained a divisive figure at his death is evident from the fact that 'not one single dignitary of the Church of England... honoured himself by being present. The Bishop, Dean and Archdeacon of the diocese were invited but none of them had even the decent courtesy to reply.'[81] With Neale's passing the future of St Margaret's now lay entirely with the women of the Sisterhood themselves.

Figure 41 *The refectory and its cloister photographed during the 1870s before the quadrangle was completed by construction of the chapel. Note the bell hanging above the wooden fence.*

In 1864, after almost of decade of leadership, Mother Ann resigned as Superior. In her place the community elected Sister Alice who was to remain as Mother until her death in 1902. Like Mother Ann, Mother Alice was one of the first women to join St Margaret's, the former in her mid-forties, the latter in her mid-twenties. Recognising Sister Alice's keen intelligence Neale made her his amanuensis and from the mid-1850s she wrote, at his dictation, in several different languages which he himself had taught her.[82] As Mother Kate later recalled, this work put her 'in touch with all his literary stores and treasures' which she freely shared with her fellow nuns.

> To be with her and to do things with her was always a special pleasure; she seemed to understand everything, and get the grasp of everything in a way few other people could, and she had a peculiar brightness which had a great charm for those who were working with her or had any dealings with her.[83]

Evidently a remarkable woman, Mother Alice was 'Marvellously large-hearted and utterly free from prejudice, she had a rare gift of insight into character, and also that special gift, the great elixir of life – a strong sense of humour.'[84]

There is no doubt that she was involved in discussions about the design of the convent and, following Neale's death, took over as the client in negotiations with architects and contractors. By August 1866 the walls were almost 6 ft high but no part of the work had yet been roofed in and the buildings were years away from completion.

It was with great joy, therefore, that the Sisterhood welcomed guests to the official opening of their new convent on St Margaret's Day, 20 July 1870. A correspondent for the *Church Times* described how the 'new building, so far as it has gone at present, forms three sides of a square, the middle portion of which, containing the chief entrance, only is completed.' The central quadrangle existed in half its intended form. Working around it, the northern wing housed the orphanage dormitories and classrooms, with sitting rooms and cubicles for three or four office-holding Sisters. In the western entrance front was the gate house with visitors' apartments, a waiting room, and oratory. In the southern portion of the quadrangle was the refectory built with the first part of the internal cloister along its northern side. Beyond it, and completing the west wing, came the kitchen, offices (ie. scullery, larder and fuel stores) and laundry.

In the gable above the entrance gate was a 'life-size stone crucifix with St Mary and St John carved in high relief by Mr. Earp who, seeing that a niche below was vacant, filled it at his own expense with a large and admirably wrought figure of the patron saint.'[85] Thomas Earp (1828-93) was based in Lambeth, where he ran the London workshop of the Earp and Hobbs partnership. His best known work is his 1863 reproduction of the Eleanor Cross which stands in Charing Cross. As a specialist in Gothic sculpture, he worked extensively with Street throughout the 1860s and 70s. Whereas George Gilbert Scott allowed his craftsmen scope to express their own style Street did not. According to Arthur Street 'If there was one thing more than another which my father would never have tolerated, it was the modification of a design by the carver, smith or whatever he might be, who was employed in carrying it out.'[86] For this reason when he found a craftsman he liked he tended to stick with him. Most of Street's ironwork was executed by James Leaver of Maidenhead who had the virtue of being both an accomplished blacksmith and churchwarden of All Saints, Boyne Hill, one of Street's most important early churches (completed 1857). It is highly likely therefore that the beautiful door hinges and other wrought ironwork throughout the Convent are Mr Leaver's work.

Figure 42 Statue of St Margaret standing in a niche by the main west entrance door, carved by Thomas Earp of Lambeth.

Figure 43

Figure 44

Figure 45

Figure 46

Street designed different hinges for all the doors in the complex which were made of wrought iron by the blacksmith James Leaver. Using the basic fleur-de-lis *motif the hinges were more or less decorative depending on their location. Figure 43 comes from the main lodge gates, figure 44 from the side door to the chapel, figure 45 from the kitchen and figure 46 from the quadrangle entrance to the Sisters' common room (now house 10).*

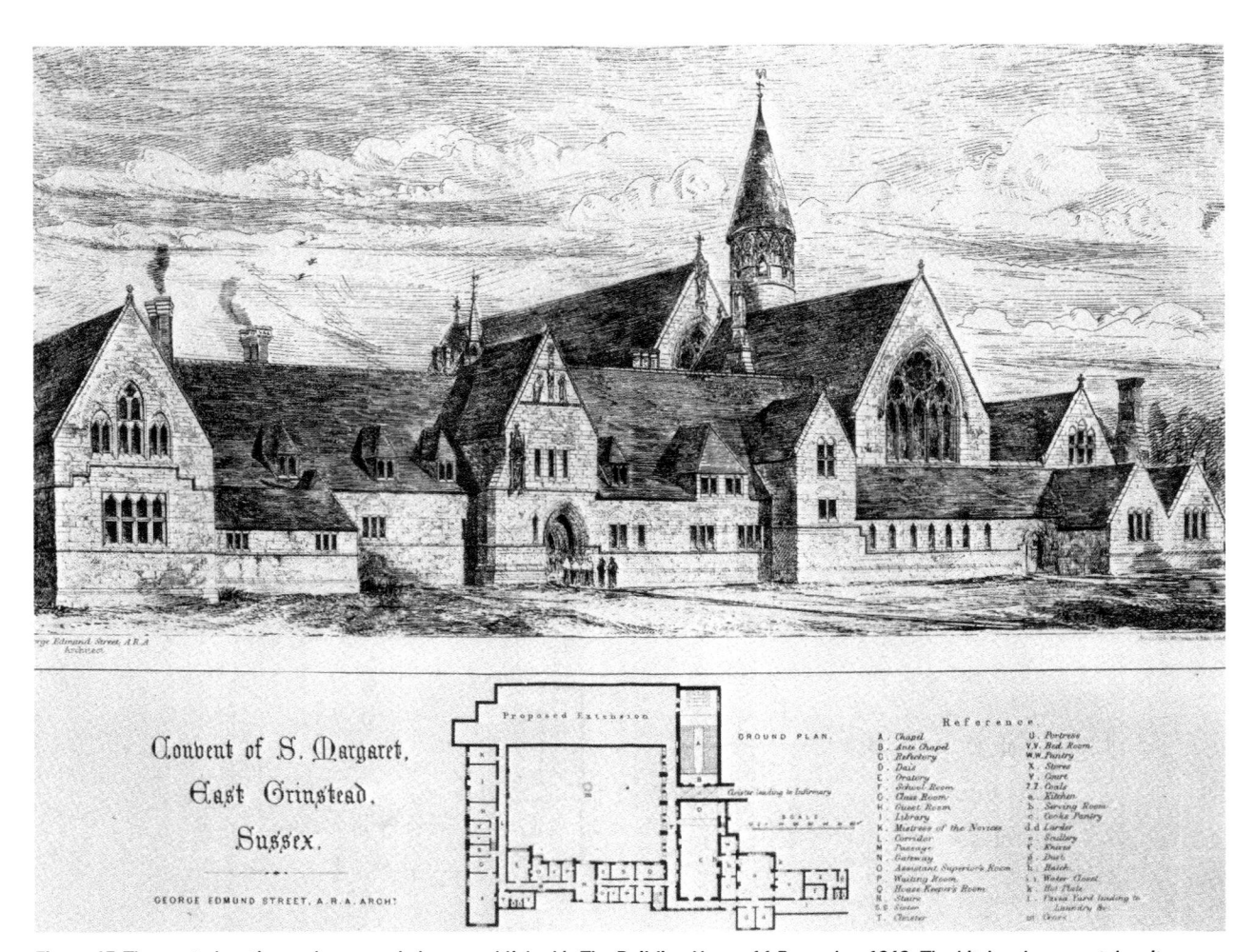

Figure 47 *The west elevation and proposed plan as published in* The Building News, *16 December 1868. The kitchen has now taken its completed form but the chapel tower is cylindrical with a conical spire. The chapel plan shows no building beyond the altar at this date.*

In 1868 G E Street published an elevation of the western range then nearing completion in the *Building News and Engineers Journal* (fig 47). A plan included beneath this engraving shows how the design was evolving with the final side of the quadrangle marked on as 'Proposed Extensions.' It also shows how the design of the kitchen had changed from 1865, when it was drawn as a square structure with pyramidal roof and turret, to the rectangular, gabled structure as built. Describing the style of the convent the sympathetic *Church Times* stated that, 'Mr Street has chosen for the refectory… [the] early second pointed, that of the remaining portion…plain first pointed, with what may be termed a dash of Sussex to give it a distinctive character.'[87] A reviewer in the *Illustrated London News,* who had seen the drawing exhibited by Street in the architecture room at the Royal Academy, was less impressed: 'The design for the Convent of St. Margaret, at East Grinstead… shows buildings nearly all roof, and with apparently less provision for light than would be found in a monastic establishment under the sun of Italy.'[88] No such criticism appears to have been levelled at the finished buildings and, in architectural history terms, Street's skill at St Margaret's lay in the way he managed to balance different elements to make a satisfying whole. In 1978 Hugh Meller of The Victorian Society praised the grand entrance front for 'its subtly placed detail creating hair's-breadth balance within the dynamic framework of asymmetrically cumulative gabled forms.' He noted how, in the quadrangle and cloister behind, Street created 'another sort of spatial harmony out of juxtaposed variety of scale and detail.'[89] Throughout the complex Street's inventiveness created a succession of richly varied exteriors. By contrast most of the interiors were strictly functional with the exception, that is, of the chapel and refectory.

In his 1955 book, *The Call of the Cloister,* Peter Anson captured something of the romance of the convent buildings when he wrote of the 'shock on entering that lofty Refectory, with its open timber roof, stone walls, encaustic tile pavement, projecting pulpit, and open fire-place – large enough for the biggest yule log ever found in the Ashdown Forest! The spacious Kitchen too evoked memories of monastic banquets such as were described by Sir Walter Scott…'[90] That the refectory boasted such proportions meant it could stand in as chapel while the real chapel was under construction. This it did for thirteen years between 1870 and 1883, with the ante-chapel in the pantry. Acknowledging this period

Figure 48 *The interior of the refectory after it had been fitted with electric light in the 1930s. The vast stone fireplace is on the left wall with the pulpit above the dias on the wall facing it. Next to this is the large stained glass window of which a detail is shown at figure 49.*

of spiritual use the Sisters continued to wear their veils in the refectory even after it took on its intended function as dining hall. Street's original drawings for a temporary wooden altar, dated April 1870, survive in the RIBA collection.[91]

Until the chapel was built the Sisters took their meals in the space subsequently divided into the tea and store rooms. Though talking was not allowed, mealtimes were accompanied by readings from the Bible or another appropriate text. For this purpose a special feature of the refectory was the pulpit, mentioned by Anson, which was raised above diners and accessed by a hidden staircase. Its design was reminiscent of the thirteenth century example still extant in the refectory at Beaulieu Abbey in Hampshire, which Street had sketched as a student in 1844.[92] The tall oriel window behind it was enriched with stained glass in 1889, the work of Bell and Beckham made possible through a legacy from Mr Charles Walker. Its emblematic designs, of the Water of Life and the Tree of Life, were chosen by Mother Alice.[93]

For all that it was unfinished, the new convent represented a big step up from the old St Margaret's Home, and proved a challenge when it came to furnishings. A 1904 article in the *St Margaret's Half-Yearly Chronicle* recalled how

> The Sisters will never forget the moving to the New House in 1870: and how the furniture which had seemed enough in the little old house looked just nothing in the large new one – and yet there was little or no money with which to supplement the old with the new. Some few things absolutely necessary were got: others had to be done without.

G E Street was well-known for his belief in the virtue of holistic design; that architecture did not stop with the exterior but should extend to every detail of a project, however small. At Cuddesdon College, for instance, he designed furniture including tables and library bookcases. It appears that large items were specially commissioned for St Margaret's but funds were lacking at the beginning and the Sisters felt some trepidation about revealing their own interior design efforts to their architect. Street was alive to their concern and, on his first visit after they had settled in, 'expressed himself as being very pleased with the taste and simplicity with which the place was furnished and arranged; and he especially admired some serge curtains which our dear Mother had chosen for the windows. Years afterwards she said how his words had encouraged her on that occasion.'[94] Notes taken from the convent diaries show

Figure 49 *The figure of St Michael as depicted in the Tree of Life window in the refectory.*

Figure 50 *The scale of the convent kitchen was comparable to that of a grand country house. Its medieval-style open crown-post roof also helped with ventilation but to cut costs the woodwork here and elsewhere was dark stained pine, reputedly from Oregon or Canada, rather than the oak one might expect. .*

that Street sent 'painted glass for the cloister' and 'Mother Kate came to paint the window of the small chapel...' Items including a piano and paintings were acquired by donation.[95]

On a practical level the move meant massive organisational changes as the community learnt to mould its daily routine to new surroundings. The convent diaries record a range of problems from the chapel roof being declared unsafe to the 'day when S Dominica went up to her room to find that the ceiling had fallen down – only minutes before.'[96] More staff had to be taken on to manage the larger site and they could also be problematic. In March 1875 Mother Alice

Figure 51 *The former convent laundry. Inside it was separated into three areas; the wash house nearest the camera had nine washing troughs, the drying room was in the centre with the ironing room at the far end.*

paid off all the laundry women, presumably after a dispute, only to find they came back the next day begging to be taken on again. Their work space was designed by Street to be as modern as possible with banks of troughs in the wash house, a drying room and laundry room with mangle and folding ironing boards. The equipment was supplied by Benham and Sons of Wigmore Street in London. The size of the laundry was a reflection of the number of women living on site but it was also fitted out in order to train the older orphans, known as Industrials, for work in service and commercial laundries.[97] When the weather allowed, laundry was hung up in the drying ground next to the embroidery workroom.

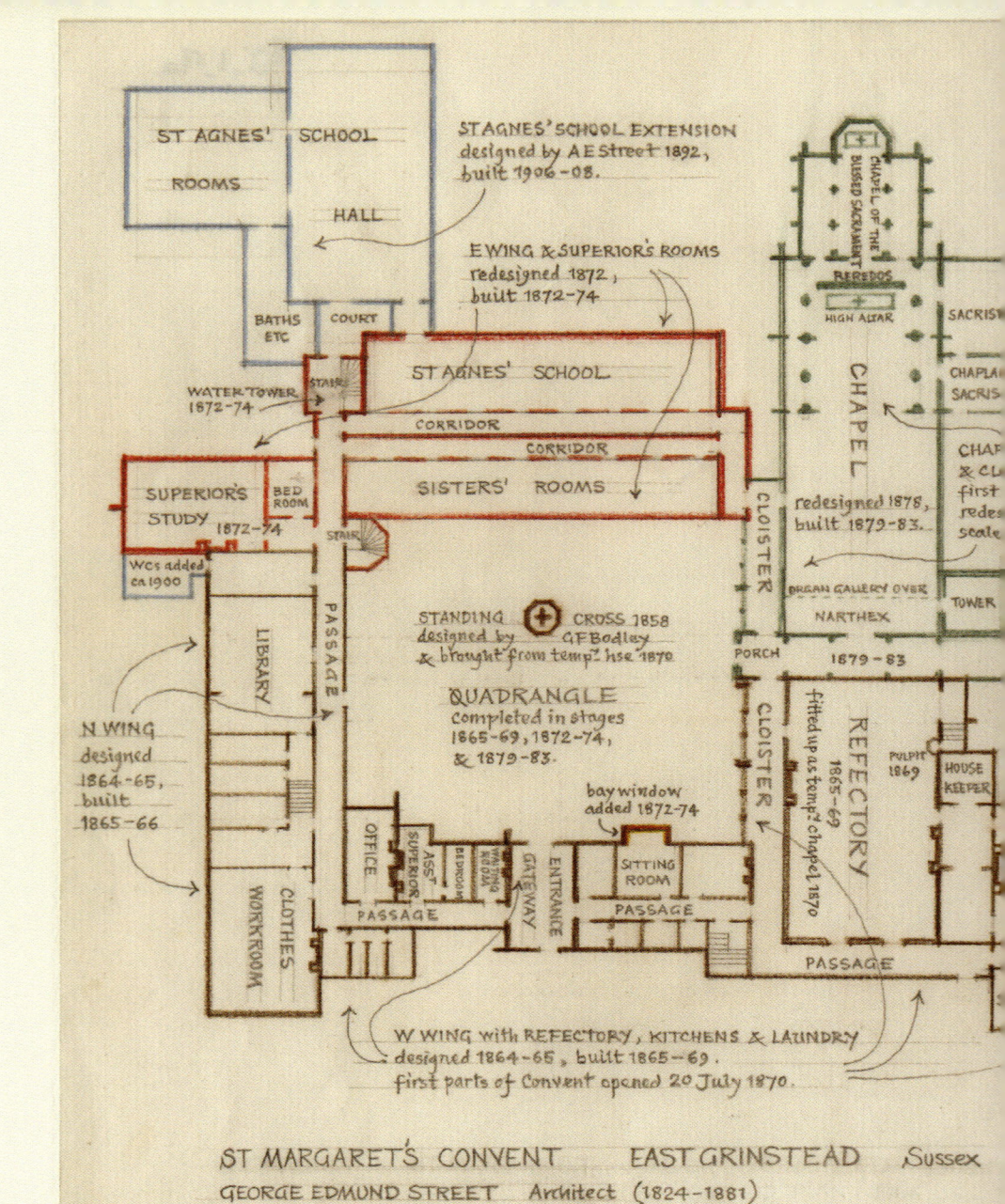

Figure 52 *This schematic ground plan, produced by architectural historian and G E Street expert Paul Joyce, shows the different phases of development at the convent.*

MAIN GATE & LODGES
designed 1870-71, built 1871-72

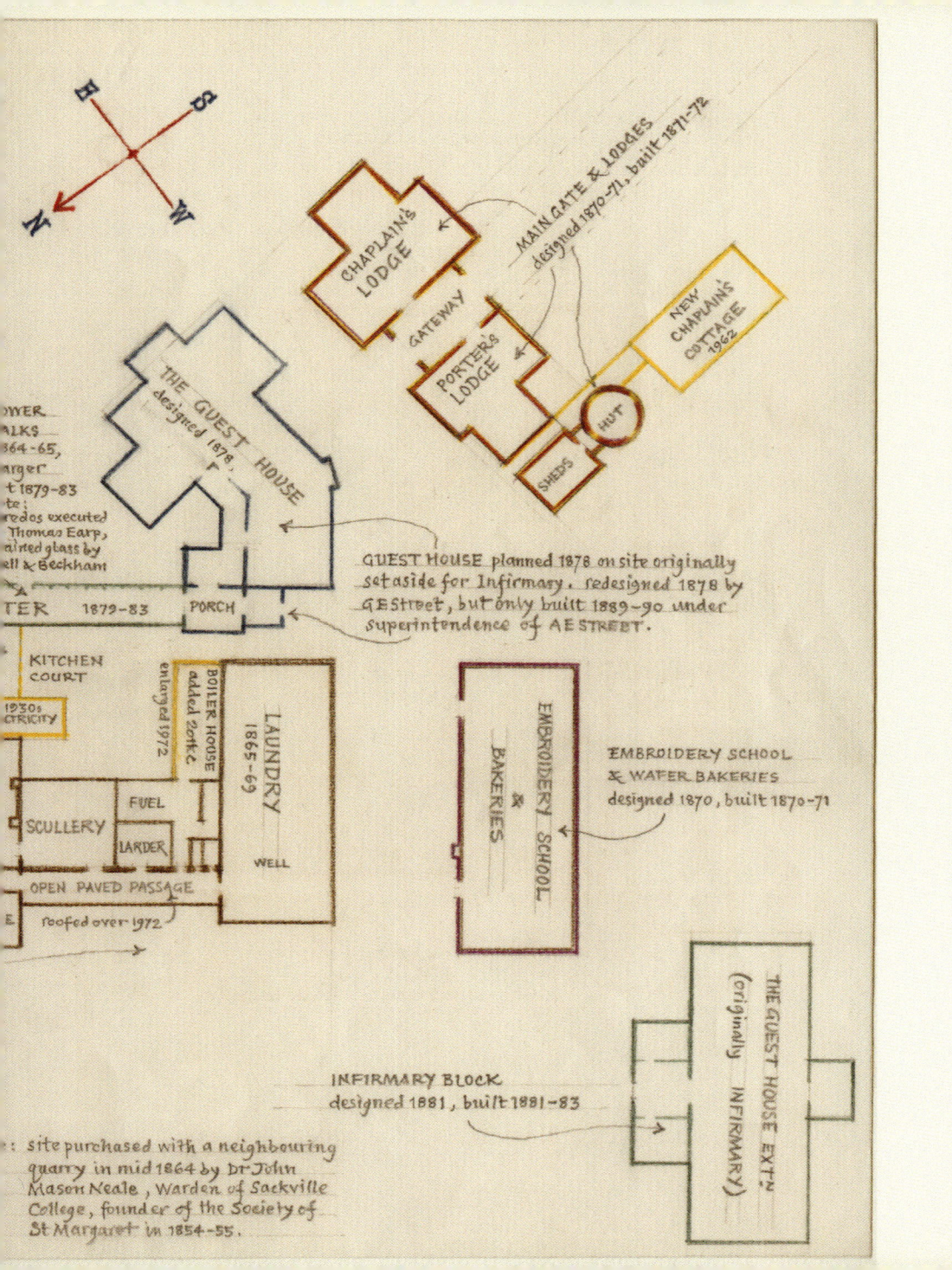

CHAPLAIN'S LODGE

GATEWAY

PORTER'S LODGE

NEW CHAPLAIN'S COTTAGE 1962

HUT

SHEDS

THE GUEST HOUSE designed 1878

...OWER
...ALKS
...864-65,
...arger
...t 1879-83
...te:
...redos executed
...Thomas Earp,
...ained glass by
...ell & Beckham

...TER 1879-83

PORCH

GUEST HOUSE planned 1878 on site originally set aside for Infirmary. redesigned 1878 by G E Street, but only built 1889-90 under superintendence of A E STREET.

KITCHEN COURT

1930s
...CTRICITY

BOILER HOUSE added 20th c. enlarged 1972

LAUNDRY 1865-69

WELL

SCULLERY

FUEL

LARDER

OPEN PAVED PASSAGE
roofed over 1972

EMBROIDERY SCHOOL & BAKERIES

EMBROIDERY SCHOOL & WAFER BAKERIES designed 1870, built 1870-71

THE GUEST HOUSE EXT^N (originally INFIRMARY)

INFIRMARY BLOCK designed 1881, built 1881-83

: site purchased with a neighbouring quarry in mid 1864 by Dr. John Mason Neale, Warden of Sackville College, founder of the Society of St Margaret in 1854-55.

Figure 53 *Ancillary buildings outside the central quadrangle formed a short street made up of the laundry and guest house (left), the chaplain's lodge and porter's lodge (centre) and embroidery workroom (right).*

For four years after the official opening, the convent remained a building site. Work continued on the embroidery workroom (built 1870-1) then the entrance gatehouse with chaplain's and porter's lodges and circular gardeners' shed (1871-2). The east ranges of the quadrangle, comprising an inner block of twenty two sisters' bedrooms, an outer block for St Agnes' School and the north east portion of the north range with Superior's room, water tower and staircase, all followed from 1872. The fact that the majority of professed Sisters had to wait several years for the completion of their sleeping accommodation and that the school also had to remain where it was while construction continued meant that it was impossible 'to give up any of the houses hiterhto occupied by the Sisterhood.' Ongoing rental of these numerous properties cost some £400 a year, the payment of which could only finally cease in 1874.[98]

In assessing the architectural merit of the ancillary buildings H S Goodhart-Rendel found them to be no less important than the main convent for, as he pointed out, 'their easy combination of stonework, timberwork, and weather-tiling, their generous roofs, their picturesque chimneys, [and] their small casements, inaugurated a period in which such things became among young architects the badge of modernity…' This was a domestic, vernacular medievalism that was to prove highly influential. At East Grinstead Street 'has brought to a convent something of the character that most of his contemporaries would have thought proper only to a farmhouse, and has sown the seed from which was to grow the profusely flowering talent of his head draughtsman, [Richard] Norman Shaw.'[99] At the convent meanwhile there was a brief period of quiet between 1874-8 as the workmen left and the first phase of building ended.

Figure 54

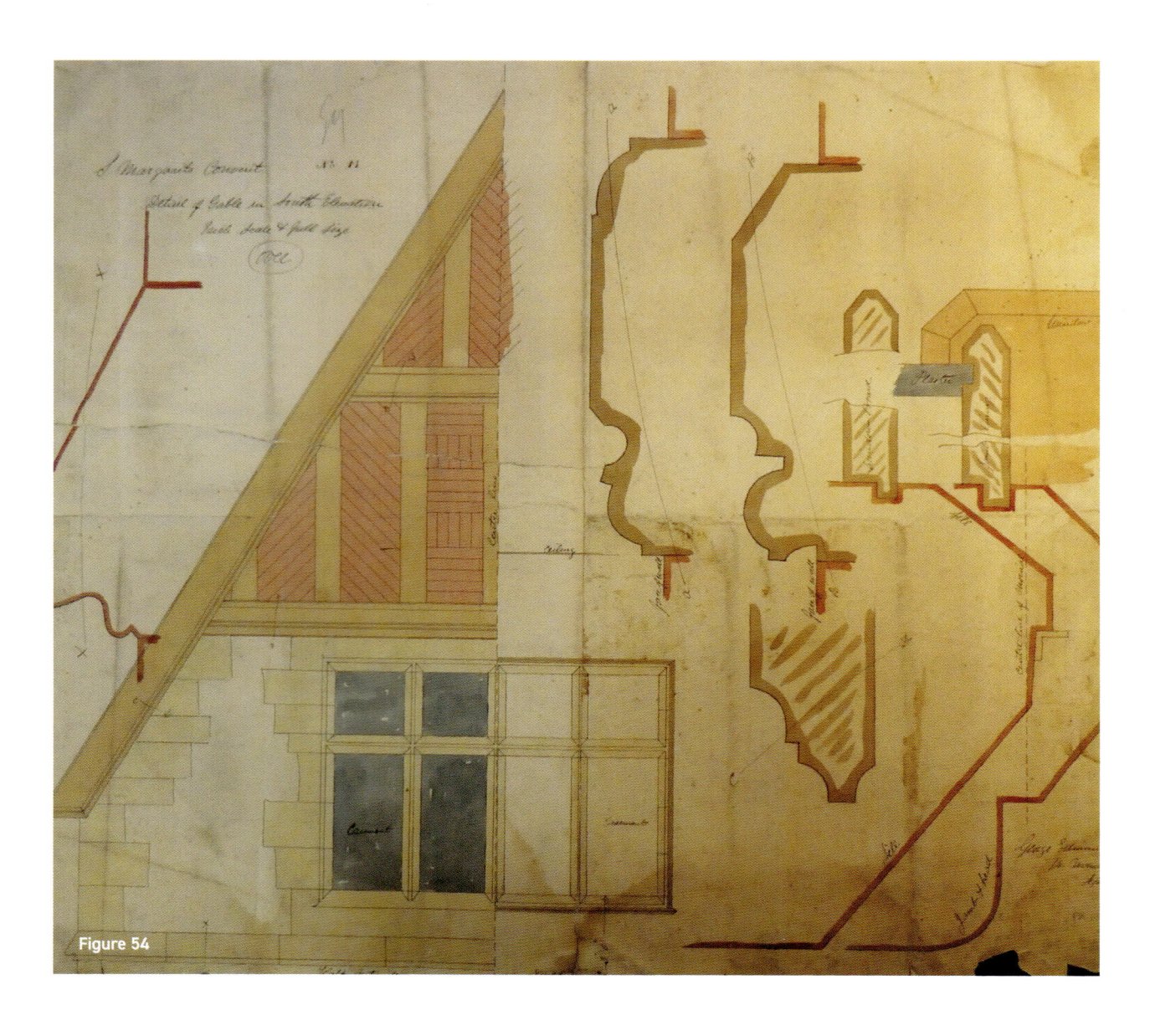

G E Street created architectural interest through the use of different materials as seen in these original drawings which combine local stone, wood and elaborate brick patterns in the gables of the chaplain's lodge (Figure 54) and orphanage dormers (Figure 55).

Figure 55

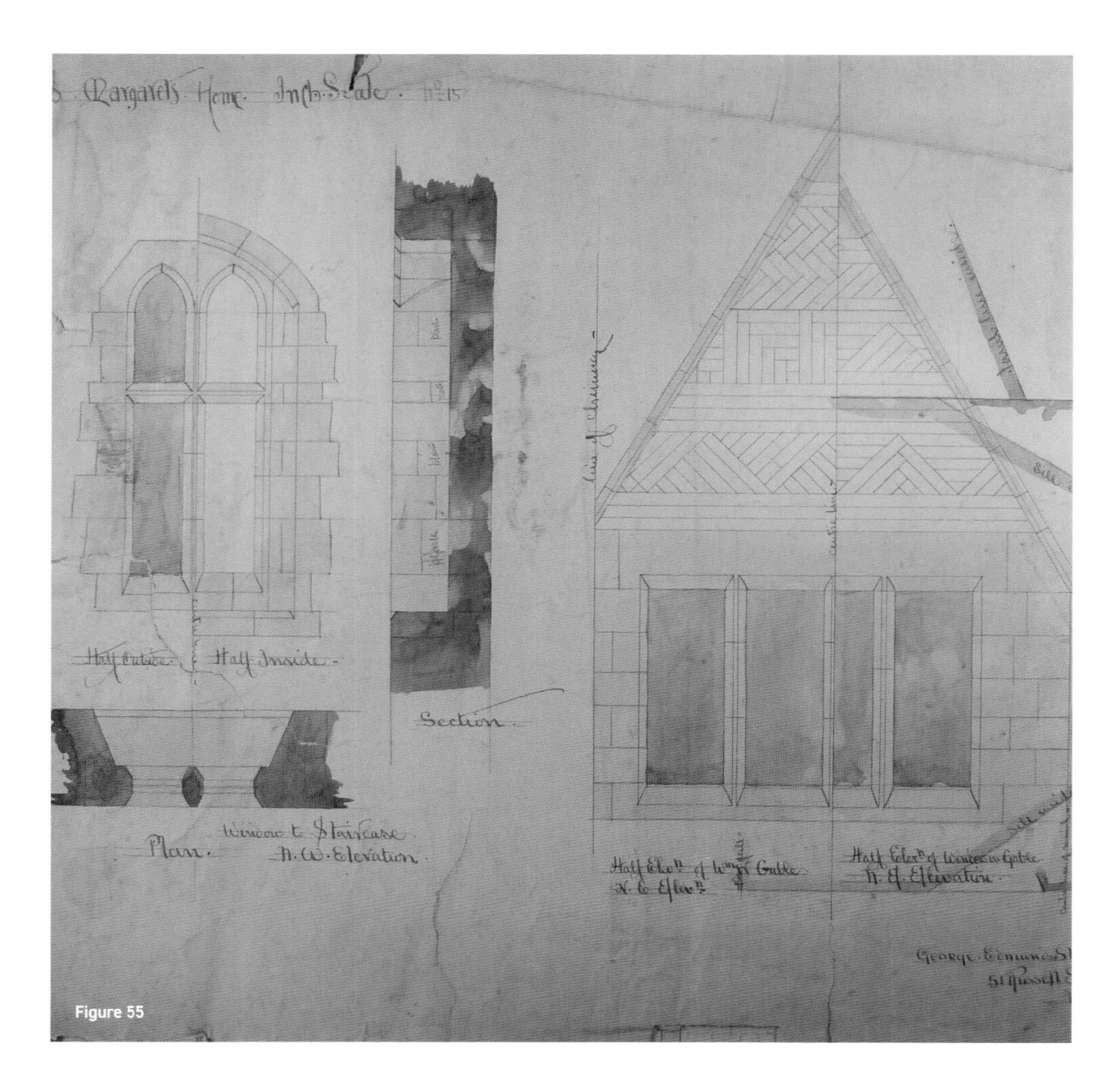

Chapter 3 The Progress of Works

Funding

In his Rules for the Society of St Margaret John Mason Neale decreed that the Sisterhood could not hold vested property or endowments. He did this to ensure there was no chance of them becoming corrupted by the accumulation of wealth, as had been the case for monastic houses before the Reformation. Neale believed that donations would be forthcoming for as long as society had need of the Sisters; when contributions ceased their mission would be complete. His vision that poverty would one day be conquered proved sadly naive and the lack of financial security it created was an ongoing challenge to the community. It was only from the 1970s that the land Neale purchased for the convent began to realise its value, ensuring the economic sustainability of the Sisterhood into the modern day.

The Sisters themselves paid a yearly fee to the community according to their means. Though the sum was set at £50 some paid more and others less. This contribution was meant principally to cover their own costs so the expenses of nursing the poor and running the orphanage had to come from donations, some of which were paid as annual subscriptions to the general fund. The additional capital expense of building the convent required a massive fundraising effort and, when finally totalled, exceeded £60,000, the greater part of which was collected in small sums.

In 1864 an appeal for £10,000 to build the Sisters 'a suitable house' was launched in the press.[100] By July 1865 they had raised £3,000, enough to begin construction but very far from sufficient. As the £713 donated on and after the foundation stone ceremony demonstrated, appeals in person were by far the most successful and if potential donors could not come to East Grinstead members of the Sisterhood were prepared to travel the country in order to seek them out. Neale used his regular lecture tours to simultaneously raise awareness and funds. He was a fine speaker and much in demand as something of a celebrity among Ritualists. In September 1865 he wrote to appraise Joseph Haskoll of his upcoming engagements:

> On Saturday, all well I go to Manchester again, to preach at the re-opening of Huntington's Church; on Monday I have a lecture on Sisterhoods at Liverpool; on Tuesday, a lecture on the ritual question at Manchester; on Wednesday, a lecture on Sisterhoods at Stafford.[101]

The following January he was back in Lancashire, giving a lecture on hymnology in Liverpool with 'expenses paid and £5 for S. Margaret's'; the day after he travelled to Wigan then back to Liverpool 'to preach at S. James the Less for S. Margaret's'.[102] Though he completed these strenuous trips and planned more it was a chill taken that bitter winter which began the final decline of his overtaxed body.

When not out nursing, members of the Sisterhood also undertook what they called 'begging' tours. As press cuttings in the St Margaret's archive demonstrate these could be very hard work, especially when people questioned their motivations. In summer 1864 Sister Lucy was in Bradford when a letter appeared in the local newspaper 'cautioning the public against a female who was soliciting subscriptions for some ecclesiastical object at East Grimstead (sic)'.[103] This situation was cleared up relatively quickly by vicar Joseph Ellis who had invited Sister Lucy to be his guest. Her subsequent visit to Burslem, however, generated daily letters to the *Staffordshire Advertiser*, for and against, for a week at the end of August. There the rector asked his brethren to beware 'A woman in the garb of a (so-called) religious order, a kind of Nun, or some such

Figure 56 *Mother Ann in outdoor garb. For a decade she undertook begging tours to raise funds for the convent building project.*

absurdity...' Hearing that the nursing Sisterhood also made 'Ecclesiastical Millinery, "Altar" cloths &c.' was too much for this low churchman and he declared in print that 'this order is altogether a Popish one, and I accordingly declined assisting the person and told her I would oppose her mission to the utmost of my power, though I shall pay for her conversion gratuitously.'[104] This does seem to have been an extreme case and other locals were ready to come to the Sisterhood's defence but fundraising like this remained an arduous task.

After Mother Ann stepped down as Superior in 1864 she split her time between begging tours and training of novices. She already had considerable fundraising experience. In December 1862 Neale recorded that she was begging in Lancashire: 'The cotton famine has, of course, been in her way: however, she has netted £200, with promises of perhaps £50 more'. As a return gesture Neale suggested Mother Ann take a Manchester orphan free of expense, which she did.[105] Her begging for the convent took her the length and breadth of the country. A surviving diary covering her tours for 1866-7 gives an insight into how the process worked. Upon arrival at a new place Mother Ann would seek out the clergy and ask for introductions to gentry and respectable local people. Little seems to have been arranged in advance so she never knew what she would find, as when she went to Brentwood in Essex on Monday 18 June 1866. The vicar was building a school so had no spare money to donate though Mr West at the Grammar School contributed £1 in spite of his own chapel building project. She travelled on to Billericay only to find the cleric there was away. A draper gave 2 shillings and told her of some church people, beyond that she had to settle for visiting the town's solicitor and leaving leaflets; 'returned to the White Hart at 8.20 with such a headache but some tea relieved it and I am able to write.' The following day she was able to send the £10 collected so far back to Mother Alice.[106]

In 1867 Mother Ann undertook two more Essex tours then raised £53 working through Northamptonshire and Lincolnshire for nine days in May. She went to Berkshire in July then spent more than a month travelling from Suffolk into Norfolk and Lincolnshire. On 1 September she noted that 'Mr Falkner, curate of Grassby, preached a good sermon about the work of women and our Sisterhood. Mr Townsend gave all the three offertories to the Building Fund, amounting to £2 7s 4d, an immense sum for their poor little Parish with only 30 houses!'[107] From there she continued north into Yorkshire then up to Newcastle and west via Harrogate and Sheffield to Wigan and Southport before returning home to East Grinstead. Sadly the sum raised during this trip is not noted but Mother Ann's expertise in this form of fundraising saw her making similar tours for some twenty years until her last was completed in November 1880. To her phenomenal effort and the kindness of strangers the convent buildings owe a huge debt.

Despite this continuing endeavour more money was always needed. Following Neale's death a memorial fund was established to raise the £25,000 required to complete phase one of building. £600 was raised on opening day in 1870 but in recording this the *Church Times* also noted that 'there is a builder's account of £1,700 to be met shortly, and a great deal more than that is required to make everything quite square so far.'[108] A mortgage was taken, payable by 1880, after which further funds had to be found for construction of the chapel. Mother Ann was by now too weak to beg and the younger nuns lacked her experience.

Thankfully the community had many wealthy patrons and Mother Alice spent a great deal of her time entertaining them. In the convent's first decade they included an Earl, seven Lords, two Knights, a Countess, a Dowager Countess, twenty Ladies and five Bishops. Some of the Sisters themselves came from aristocratic families: Sister Maria was Lady Emily Somers-Cocks and Sister Evelyn was Lady Evelyn Moreton. 'Their families were constant visitors and became great friends of the Community. S. Zillah's father was a knight-herald living in the shadow of St Paul's Cathedral.'[109] Other supporters who did not feel able to commit fully to the life became Associates. This role was instituted in 1858 and ensured that the Sisters had a network of people ready to help them outside of the convent. Associates were mostly female but key male friends were also made Priests Associate and Brothers Associate. All gave as much financial help as they could while saying daily prayers for the Sisters and their work. It was thanks to the generous gift of £5000 from Associate and benefactor Charlotte Rosa Raine that work could finally begin on the chapel in 1878.[110]

Figure 57 *Published engraving of the perspective view exhibited by Street at the Royal Academy in 1879. At this time the chapel and guest house were under construction. A cemetery was still envisaged to the south of the chapel and the infirmary was not shown.*

Phase Two: 1878-1900

Designs for St Margaret's Convent evolved over time. Once in occupation, the Sisters were able to specify their requirements more accurately but details also changed in response to Street's developing architectural style. The most altered element was the chapel tower which looked different in each of the three published designs, having a pointed roof with gargoyles and crockets in 1865, a circular turret in 1868 and its final saddleback roof a decade later. This roof shape was to become a favoured detail of Street's later church architecture. In his final scheme Street also introduced a guest house to stand on the site formerly proposed for the infirmary, connecting with the chapel by a covered walkway. The infirmary itself was relocated to the south west of the embroidery workshop, at a sensible distance from the main complex. Work began there in 1881. Construction of the guest house had to wait until the end of the decade.

In 1879 Street exhibited his perspective view of the convent at the Royal Academy. This drawing, which was subsequently published in the building press, showed the site from the east emphasising the scale of the new chapel to be built at its centre. Street's son wrote that the original drawing was '34 inches by 22, a

Figure 58 *The marble and alabaster reredos, carved by Thomas Earp, is framed by columns made of Kilkenny marble. These and the vaulted ceiling they support were the gift of G E Street.*

Figure 59 *Original contract drawings for the chapel dated July 1878 and signed by the contractors Wall and Hook. Note the proposed east end of the guest house in stone with pointed windows that echo the treatment of the chapel.*

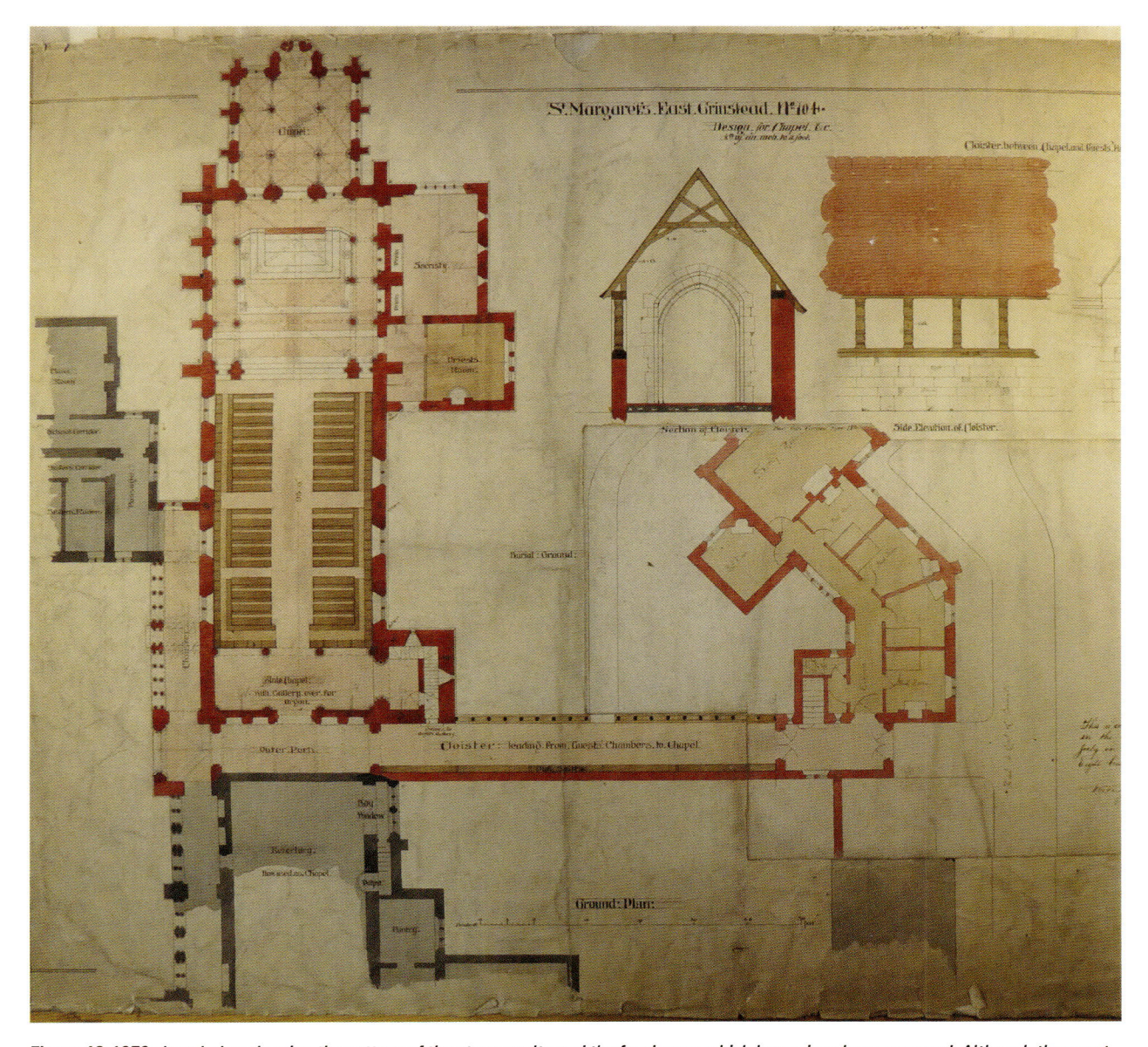

Figure 60 *1878 chapel plan showing the pattern of the stone vaults and the fixed pews which have since been removed. Although the guest house is shown in its final dog-leg plan this is the result of a new design having been stuck over the original.*

Figure 61 *Despite its small size the eastern chapel is arguably the most beautiful space in the convent with its encaustic tiled floor and nine vaulted compartments.*

very fair size, and full of buildings all running at odd angles to each other, and consequently presenting an unusual quantity of work for the amount of paper to be covered.' It was made over four nights, taking a mere sixteen hours to complete and 'Any one who remembers the drawing will allow this to be remarkably quick.'[111] It should also be kept in mind that the aerial viewpoint was entirely Street's mental visualisation since this was an epoch before aeroplanes and thus aerial photography.

The chapel's foundation stone was laid on 23 July 1879 by Francis Barchard, using the same silver trowel presented to him at the original ceremony of 1865. This time the contractors were Wall and Hook from Brimscombe in Gloucestershire, a firm of stonemasons who specialised in church-building with prior experience of working on Street and Bodley commissions. Wall and Hook estimated the first part of the chapel (shell, lower part of tower, sacristies, cloister walk with porch into quadrangle and chapel cloister) to take two years and cost £10,000.

On the annual St Margaret's Day celebration in July 1881 Street made his last visit to the convent with his son 'to see how things looked.'

Figure 62 *This stone panel depicting St Margaret is one of three monochrome insets in the tiled floor of the eastern chapel. The others depict Eucharistic symbols.*

Chapter 3 The Progress of Works 99

Despite his considerable fame, Street 'had a natural horror of being made much of in his own person' and surrounded by, as he put it, 'a great mob of people', he left the event before the speeches began.[112] From this time onward Street's health began to fail, the result of overwork and the stress of bureaucratic wranglings necessitated by his most famous work, the Royal Courts of Justice in London's Strand. When he died on 18 December he was Treasurer and Professor of Architecture at the Royal Academy, President of the Royal Institute of British Architects (RIBA), a member of the Academy of Vienna and a Knight of the French Legion of Honour. Though he was just fifty seven and his 'robust physique' might have suggested the possibility of a long life, the *Church Times* was not alone in noting that, 'in point of fact, if measured by his works, he had already spent one.' The list of his original works and restorations extends over ten pages in the back of his son's *Memoir*, and it was said that 'for the Law Courts alone he made no fewer than three thousand working drawings with his own hand!'[113] A collection of original drawings for the East Grinstead convent survives in the archive of the RIBA though it is clear these are but a small proportion of those he actually produced. Street's son, Arthur Edmund (1855-1938), took on the job of completing his father's outstanding projects but noted that 'it is rare, indeed, for me to meet a client of his who does not cherish his memory as a man and as an artist.' As late as 1911, an article in the *Half-Yearly Chronicle* referred to him as 'our own Mr Street.'[114]

In 1883 the infirmary was completed and on 26 July the chapel and cloisters were opened. Elizabeth Williamson writes of the chapel exterior in the 2019 Pevsner: 'It is very tall with long, slender two-light windows in the nave, single-light windows in the chancel, a long, even, tiled roof, and a bold, slim and high tower on the S side, crowned by a saddleback roof such as Street liked, and with exceedingly long bell-openings...'[115] Peter Anson declared that it ought to be considered a church because 'it was too large and stately to be called a chapel – had Mr Street,' he asked, 'ever designed anything so devotional?'[116] The effect of the high, open interior is quite astonishing, with attention directed to the large and splendid reredos in the chancel. To either side, this is framed by tall columns of Irish black marble, the cost of which was borne by Street himself. Buttressed by the outside walls, these columns allow an uninterrupted view of the east end with its vaulted stone ceiling, also paid for by Street.

Figure 63 *One of the fifty four misereres carved by Sr Edith. It took her seven years to create this unique set of birds, beasts and flora.*

The marble and alabaster reredos was carved to Street's designs by Thomas Earp and paid for by one of the Sisters. In front of it, the alabaster altar with Greek marble pillars, was also the work of Earp, the gift of Fr Alison in memory of his mother. The candlesticks and Crucifix that originally sat upon the altar were again designed by Street. The east rose window was dedicated to the memory of Mother Ann who, having died in May 1881, never got to see the chapel completed; the centre light, emblematical of the Seven Sacraments, was given by the pupils of St Agnes' School.[117]

Invisible from the main chapel, and accessed through 'pencil-thin arches into narrow passages' behind the chancel arch, is the Chapel of the Blessed Sacrament otherwise known as the Eastern or Lady Chapel (fig 61).[118] This chapel did not appear on the plans published in 1868 but performed an important function as the location of the Reserved Sacrament, which was housed there in a decorated tabernacle. The continuing need for secrecy around this controversial practice no doubt explains the sensation of this being a hidden space. Williamson describes it as 'an exquisite Dec[orated] miniature', that is to say in a style inspired by English Gothic architecture of c1290 to c1350. There are 'Nine vaulted compartments on four clustered shafts, a small vaulted apse with blind arcaded walls and an alabaster altar facing the equally rich cusped entrance arch and traceries opening to the Chapel.' The floor is laid with a complex pattern of marble and encaustic tiles, some of the latter featuring Eucharistic symbols. The three lights in the east window were given by Clemency Blatherwick, an Associate member of St Margaret's. The three lights on the north side of the chapel show British saints with those on the south side depicting Virgin saints.[119]

Figure 64 *Fr Laughton Alison was convent chaplain for twenty five years from 1867.*

To begin with the lancet windows in the nave of the main chapel were clear but by 1895 all had been filled with stained glass from the workshop of Bell and Beckham at 98 Great Russell Street, London. The last three to be completed were given in memory of Fr Alison by his family, the community and the townspeople respectively. After John Mason Neale's death the Sisterhood chose the Rev Fr La Barte to replace him as their spiritual guide. His appointment was not a success and the position of Chaplain remained vacant until in March 1867, the Rev Laughton Alison came to visit. His family were from Chorley in Lancashire but after graduating from Cambridge University he became curate at Cuckfield in Sussex. Only intending to stay at St Margaret's for a few weeks, the thirty-one year old proved such a good fit that he ended up staying until his death on 19 September 1892. The Edwardian historian of East Grinstead, Wallace H. Hills, deemed Alison to be a worthy successor to Neale; 'a man of sincere piety, of wide general information and cheerfulness of spirit; eloquent in speech and kindly in manner..' Though viewed with suspicion at first because of his advanced views he helped influence local opinion in favour of the Sisterhood. 'Certain it is, that for all his retiring habits, and almost unconnected as he was with the parochial life of East Grinstead, he somehow came to be known and held in affectionate esteem by all classes in the town, and on the day of his quiet funeral the place seemed hushed in general mourning for a well-loved friend.'[120] Fr Alison was succeeded as Chaplain by the Rev Reginald Ernest Hutton. Hutton's father was an Evangelical priest living at Felbridge when Neale came to Sackville College and it was he who denounced Neale to the Bishop causing his inhibition from preaching. According to Neale's biographer, A G Lough, Hutton considered his thirty-three year commitment to the convent as 'an act of reparation for the wrong his family had done to Dr. Neale.'[121]

Like the chapel windows, the decoration of the oak choir stalls was undertaken after completion of the building. The *Half-yearly Chronicle* for January 1904 reported that 'It is seven years since Sister Edith brought her chisel to bear upon the first of the fifty-four "Miserere", and each in turn has been removed to her workshop to be there carved by her, in high relief, with exquisite carvings of birds – and beasts – and open flowers – the design in no two cases being the same.'[122] Sister Edith was born Edith Maud Mason in Essex, c1850 and clearly had considerable artistic talent. Her designs included native bird species, fruits such as strawberries and pomegranates, as well as a more exotic elephant and pair of giraffes. In 1905 these were under threat when the flooring in the Sisters' stalls was discovered to be uneven due to the joists and other oak work becoming rotten from damp which had been penetrating the wall from the cloister outside. For a period of five weeks the Sisters were deprived of twelve seats as well as the section where visitors usually sat in order that the woodwork there could be completely renewed. Investigations showed that the original builders had only laid a thin layer of cement between the blocks of wood and the earth 'and for some time labourers were employed in digging out clay which was carried out in sacks!' To prevent the damp recurring substantial work had to be done in the quadrangles which were thoroughly drained and fitted with stone gutters. As the report on this work ruefully concluded, this whole process 'Required much underground work to satisfy the architect and will loom large in this year's accounts.'[123] In 1926 repair work had to be undertaken to the roofs of the chapel and refectory cloisters, after the wood-work under the tiles there was found to be rotten.[124] As such examples demonstrate, the expense of the convent did not end with its completion.

The final element of the Neale memorial complex was the guest house, the foundation stone for which was was not laid until July 1889. When G E Street produced the drawing illustrated at fig 59 in 1878, the building looked quite different. A linear block on the same orientation as the chapel, it was to be an entirely stone structure with a flat eastern elevation punctuated by differing sets of the same Gothic-style lancet windows. Within a year this design had given way to a more interesting dog-leg plan that featured a mix of different materials on its façades. Ultimately executed by A E Street after his father's death, the guest house went through further alterations whilst remaining faithful to the spirit of the 1879 design. A comparison of the elder Street's perspective view from that year (fig 57) and the design published by Arthur Street in *The Building News* in 1890 (fig 65), also exhibited at the Royal Academy shows the addition of a full-height bay on the east end of the building. This was actually constructed to first-floor height only, an adjunct to the ground floor sitting room. As with the chapel, the building contractors were Wall and Hook who charged £2922 17s. Local Hackenden stone was combined with an upper storey of half-timbered oak work with tile-hanging in the gable creating a finished effect wholly in keeping with the

Vernacular Revival G E Street had helped to inaugurate. Inside, the rooms were accessed off a corridor connected to the cloister; the ground floor was laid with 'Gregory's wood blocks on concrete.'[125] After it was opened on 5 October 1900 the guest house was used by poor people seeking help, rich Associates on retreat and women thinking of joining the Order.

Completion of the guest house might have meant the end of the Street connection with the Sisterhood but that Mother Alice had made it one of her last business arrangements to 'secure Mr [Arthur] Street's aid in the important matter of taking charge of the Convent buildings and in superintending the repairs which year by year are found to be necessary and cannot with safety be postponed.' In 1903 'Our valued friend' Mr Arthur Street retired from architectural practice. As an only child he had gone into the profession to please his father but chose now to focus on his true loves of literature, art and

Figure 65 *A E Street's design for the guest house was published in* The Building News, *June 1890.*

Figure 66 *The guest house exterior is a mix of timber framing, tile hanging and stonework, a palette of materials that demonstrates Street's sensitivity to local building traditions.*

music; according to his obituary Street was an 'exceptionally fine baritone singer.'[126] He passed on the job at St Margaret's to John Carrington Stockdale (1861-1949) who had worked with him for many years; 'The knowledge that we can at once obtain his advice and experienced attention on all these matters very much lessens the weight of responsibility in this respect.'[127] Just as important was the fact that through Stockdale the original link back to G E Street was maintained into the 1920s.

Stockdale had joined the elder Mr Street's practice in 1877 working on the staff at the Royal Courts of Justice. Of a similar age to Arthur Street he stayed with him after his father's death, taking on the role of manager in the firm. He ran his own practice from 1901 and from the list of his works it seems his principal client was the Society of St Margaret's for whom he worked as consulting architect to the Order's Hostel of God at Clapham Common as well as the Mother House at East Grinstead.[128] Stockdale was continually called upon to maintain the convent and in 1903 was charged with installing new fire escapes throughout the complex following the recent fatal fire at Eton College. That same year also saw him reorganise the convent gasworks. A novelty upon their construction in the 1860s, the private gasworks were important for the Sisters self-sufficiency. At that date they would have been used for lighting only, since gas central heating had yet to be developed and the kitchen ranges, laundry boilers and fireplaces were all fuelled by coal. Though the gasworks were renewed the installation of heating was piecemeal and not fully accomplished until the 1930s. Such maintenance issues were chiefly the concern of the Mother Superior but the next chapter looks at how the Sisters lived and worked together at St Margaret's.

Figure 67 This published portrait of A E Street cites him as architect of Halifax Cathedral in Canada. He held the post of convent architect until his retirement in 1903.

Figure 68 The guest house and chapel were linked by the enclosed cloister seen here. The girls in straw hats are Edwardian pupils of St Agnes' School.

Figure 69 *Detail of the high altar festal frontal designed by John Sedding and worked by the Society of St Margaret for presentation to the Dean and Chapter of York Minster in 1869. This panel, with its stylised Arts and Crafts foliage, depicts the paradise of God.*

Chapter 4
Convent Life

Living at St Margaret's

Life in the convent was defined by simplicity and routine; no one had more than anyone else and everyone knew what was expected of them. From the Mother Superior to the newest novice, every Sister was required to abide by the Rule. This code of conduct, devised by John Mason Neale and based upon medieval precedents, united women from different parts of the country and with different backgrounds into a cohesive community with shared goals. As an illustration of the geographical reach of St Margaret's reputation, among the twenty six professed Sisters at the Mother House on census day, 3 April 1881, there were women from Cumberland, Yorkshire, Derbyshire, Staffordshire, Devon and Dorset, as well as the nearer counties of Middlesex, Surrey and Kent. Their average age was forty one.[129]

Becoming a nun required extensive training and those applicants inspired by the Victorian craze for all things medieval and pseudo-Gothic rarely made it through the stringent selection process. This began with a letter to the Mother Superior then, following an interview, the invitation to spend a few weeks living in the convent as a visitor. An 1867 essay intended for young women contemplating this first trial period prepared them for what they would find on arrival:

A lay Sister, or an orphan, or in some case the Senior Sister then at home, opens the door, and the dress strikes you immediately. You have no objection to distinctive dress, or you would scarcely have come so far; and you will soon see plainly enough for yourself how absolutely needful it is. Then, although there is a good thick door-mat, you see no vestige of carpet; the nearest approach to which is cocoa-nut matting, and there is not a great deal of that. The furniture and fittings are mostly stained deal; so are the floors, unless they are left unstained, with no other adornment than scrubbing. You must not speak on the stairs or in the passages; therefore follow, if you please, in silence, while you are led to your room. It is small, you see, but large enough to turn about in, particularly as during your stay you will wear no crinoline. You have an iron bedstead, a mattress, and plenty of blankets, conveniences for washing, a press for clothes, a chair, and perhaps a table, and a piece of matting on the floor. On the walls are prints of religious subjects; possibly, also, illuminations, and some text painted as a cornice round the room. You will, if you please, wear a little net or muslin cap while you visit at this house, and if your dress is black or grey, so much the better.[130]

By the 1870s middle and upper class homes were already very colourful places, full of the wares of Victorian mass-production including bright wallpapers, fitted carpets and an ever-growing array of knick-knacks. Clothing had also been transformed by the introduction of aniline dyes yet, as the above quote makes plain, the results of this burgeoning consumer culture were conspicuously absent from the convent setting. Moving into St Margaret's meant accepting a genuine reduction in living standards and the extreme bareness of the living accommodation shocked some visitors.

Those women not put off by this contrast served six months as a postulant, helping in the work of the community, sharing its devotions and getting to know the philosophy, rules and personnel of the House. At the end of this term they could proceed to the novitiate only if the community

Figure 70 *A group of novices photographed c1895.*

two Orders and established a single Choir Order throughout the Society of St Margaret.

Novices took on a new name (often a version of their given name) prefixed by 'Sister' and began their training in earnest. Under the care of the Novice Mistress they gained a grounding in Christian doctrine which was enhanced by rigorous academic study. Maintaining the high standards set by their Founder, the curriculum for East Grinstead novices included St Augustine in English, ecclesiastical history in French and translation from Latin. Alongside this they pursued a practical education that would allow them to become effective nurses and teachers. For Choir Sisters brought up in households full of servants this began with the domestic basics of laying a fire, scrubbing a floor and boiling a saucepan of water.

In theory, a Sister could remain a novice indefinitely but the ultimate goal was to be professed as a Sister for life. This required a positive vote from two-thirds of the already professed Sisters and even at this stage rejection rates remained high. To commit fully to convent life meant taking the vows of chastity, poverty and obedience. These vows ensured that a Sister had no competing loyalties; she agreed

Figure 71 *Novices Francesca and Veronica captured outside the laundry as they go about their daily chores in the 1960s.*

voted in their favour. In most convents between a third and a half of applicant novices were rejected, though some were accepted on later attempts. In 1881 the census recorded six postulants and nine novices at East Grinstead. The latter were divided into Choir sisters from wealthy backgrounds who served two years and Lay sisters, from the respectable working class, who served double that. This division continued until 1935 when modernising Mother Madeleine abolished the

Figure 72 *Floral bouquets and head garlands were used to mark the day that Sisters were professed for life. The Sisters in this photograph probably came from St Margaret's, Colombo.*

Figure 73 *An original convent key now in the collection of East Grinstead Museum.*

to be obedient to the Rule otherwise how would the community operate, she agreed to give up her money because the Sisterhood promised to keep her and she agreed to be chaste because she could not devote herself fully to God if she also had a husband, and any other relationship would be a sin. Such vows were understood to be demanding, hence the long training period. Yet the Sisters were given far greater chance for reflection and release than the millions of Victorian women who made their marriage vows, also committing themselves for life, without any trial period or possibility of escape in an age when divorce was almost impossible.

Key decisions about membership and policy were taken in Chapter by vote amongst the Sisters. On a daily basis, however, it was the Mother Superior who led the community and shouldered the responsibilities of a large national, and increasingly international, organisation. Part chief executive she was also, as her title proclaimed, a mother figure to the women, children and workers bound to the community. Hers was an elected position yet all the women who assumed the role of Mother did so over numerous re-elections. Mother Ann stepped down before the convent was built so from its opening in 1870 until its sale in 1976 just five Sisters took charge of its running: Mother Alice (1864-1902), Mother Ermenild (1902-32), Mother Madeleine (1932-45), Mother Geraldine Mary (1945-58) and Mother Gabriel (1958-76). The Mother Superior had no secular equivalent in Victorian society and even during most of the twentieth century her position of authority remained unusual. She was accorded the same reverence as church dignitaries and had the right to appoint her Assistant Superior, Bursar and Novice Mistress. Beyond this hierarchy in the Mother House, there were opportunities for the brightest women to take charge of mission work elsewhere, providing roles with an exceptional degree of independence to those who wanted them.

Outside the convent, routines were shaped by the Sisters' nursing or teaching work. Inside it was the round of chapel services that defined daily life. A typical convent day in the 1870s might take the following form:

6am	Rise
6.50	Office of Prime
7am	Celebration of Holy Eucharist
8am	Breakfast
8.30	Make bed and dust room
9am	Office of Terce
10-12	School
12 noon	Office of Sext, and Meditation in the Oratory
1pm	Dinner
1.30-2.30	Recreation Hour
2.30-3.10	Meditation in Oratory and Office of Nones
3.10-5	Needlework or Study
5	Office of Vespers
5.30	Tea
6-8.45	Needlework or Night School etc followed by
7.15	Office of Compline and
8.45	Supper
9.15	Office of Anticipated Matins
11	In bed.[131]

Figure 74 *Sketch of the diminutive bell-turret on the inner face of the gate arch into the quadrangle by artist and Old Convent resident Susan Quekett.*

Figure 75 *Sr Mabel feeding the chickens. Professed in 1870, Sr Mabel spent forty years as a Sister working in Wigan and London's Queen Square before failing health sent her back to the convent. She died in 1912.*

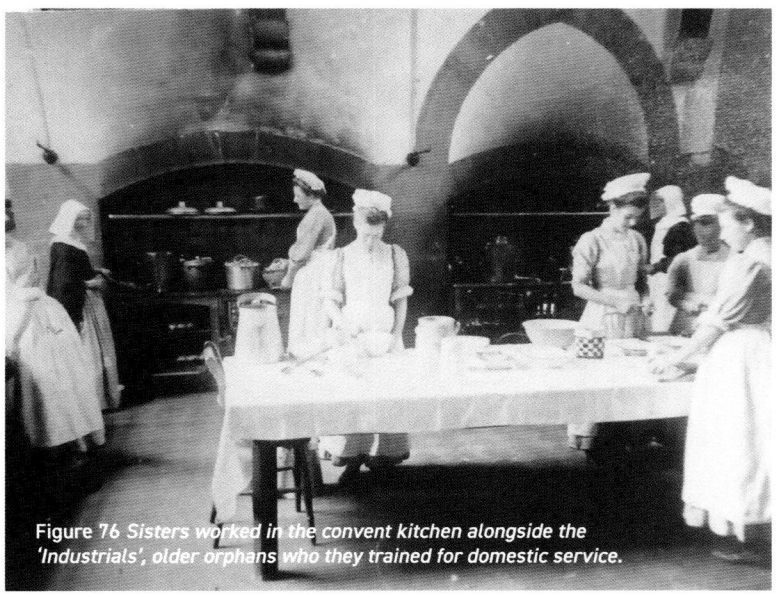

Figure 76 *Sisters worked in the convent kitchen alongside the 'Industrials', older orphans who they trained for domestic service.*

Figure 77 *Sr Elsa in the kitchen garden which supplied food for the community.*

Chapter 4 Convent Life

This schedule was measured out by the toll of the bell which is still housed in the small, slender turret above the quadrangle.

Such a method of communal time keeping reached everyone on the convent site. This originally included seven full-time gardeners, laundresses and needlewomen. In the kitchen there were cooks who were assisted by up to twenty five Industrials, later known as St Lucy's girls, whose labour made a huge difference to the successful running of the convent. By the turn of the century the daily average of those sitting down to meals in the refectory was 200, made up of Sisters, school pupils and orphans. On St Margaret's Day the room held 240 for luncheon. As much food as possible was grown on site with photographs showing extensive vegetable and potato plots which must have been tended by the gardeners. The Sisters also kept chickens and a field for pigs at the eastern corner of their land. Meals were simple reflecting the Sisters' vow of poverty and when money was short portions had to be rationed. Unlike for the poor people they helped, however, it was 'regularly supplied, of adequate amount and acceptable, if not excellent, quality.'[132] Sylvia Spencer, who grew up in the orphanage during the 1920s, remembered breakfast of sweetened porridge, followed by 'bread and scrape', either margarine or dripping with marmalade or jam, and hot milk and water served in a white enamel jug.'[133]

Within the Sisters' daily routine there were dedicated times for silence. This was not meant to stifle discussion, rather to provide a space for individual contemplation. Relaxation was also prioritised. From the outset Neale recognised that the difficulty of the tasks allotted to the Sisters would necessitate some light relief. As a novelist himself, he advocated reading fiction, albeit from a carefully selected range of suitable titles. The convent gardens also provided welcome sanctuary. Sister Kate, by then Mother of the Priory of the Holy Cross at Haggerston, recalled walking among them on one lovely November visit to East Grinstead:

> The alleys of quaint old-fashioned espalier apple-trees were, of course, brown and bare; but there was a "gallant walk" bordered by huge dahlias, each one growing like a burning bush, with every shade you can imagine – of claret, crimson, flame-colour, pink, orange, purple and the delicatest mauve, white and the sweetest yellows – all that the heart could desire.[134]

Figure 78 *Headstones in the convent cemetery. The grave decorated with flowers is that of Mother Ermenild who died in 1932.*

Space was set aside in the convent for communal recreation and whether they talked, wrote letters, played chess or did needlework there was always a sense of togetherness in the room. Neale also specified that 'The Sisters shall have free intercourse with their parents or their brothers and sisters at any time...' With approval of the Mother Superior other relations and friends could visit too.[135] The earliest version of the St Margaret's Rule allowed the Sisters to take up to two months away from the convent each year to visit family or travel. The latter was often done in parties and on one notable sketching trip to the Continent the Superiors of East Grinstead and Clewer were joined by several Sisters and Associates of their relative communities.

Convent life had to encompass death, a very real risk for those who went out to nurse people suffering from the worst diseases in the most squalid conditions. The convent infirmary was built to provide an on-site nursing facility and, separate from the main complex, could be used to quarantine nuns and children suffering from contagious diseases. Elderly sisters nearing the end often enjoyed the peace and sea air of St Catherine's Home at Ventnor, Isle of Wight, which was run by the community as a hospital for incurable tuberculosis cases. It was there that Mother Alice died from heart failure aged seventy-two. At first no special provision was available for burial of the Sisters. An 1870 report in the *Church Times* noted that two of

Figure 79 *The imposing carved Pieta was installed in the cemetery in 1907 and remains there today.*

them were buried with Neale in St Swithun's churchyard, alongside orphans and a workman, William Wood Thornton, who had died during construction of the convent.[136] By the time Mother Ann died there were dedicated plots for the Sisters at the town cemetery, opened on West Hill in 1869.

It was not until 12 October 1892, that ground within the convent was consecrated for cemetery use. G E Street's original designs included a burial garth within the convent precinct, behind the refectory and kitchen, but there is no evidence this space was ever used in such a way. When the cemetery was finally created, it was away from the main buildings in a wooded vale unsuitable for vegetable cultivation. This area was cleared by the gardening staff who also built a wooden mortuary chapel there. According to the inscribed stone slabs which survive in the cemetery the first burial happened in 1899 when Lay Novice, Sister Edna was interred. In June 1902 she was joined by Mother Alice, the coffin carried from the funeral service in the main chapel via the cloister and out of the great gateway, into 'that little wood which Mother was so specially fond of.' Mother Alice was laid to rest 'at the top of a little slope just opposite the Crucifix.[137] Forty-six local firms sent flowers and messages of sympathy.[138] In 1903 her Assistant Superior, Sister Lucy was buried in the neighbouring plot.

In 1907 a 9 foot-high Pieta was erected at the southern end of the cemetery. In the centre of this *bas relief* sculpture the Virgin Mary cradles the dead body of Jesus Christ with an angel to either side. The intention was to make this a memorial stone to all members of the Sisterhood who had passed away, whether at the Mother House or Daughter Houses around the world, though the plan of inscribing names on the rear was never carried out. Burials in the cemetery continued for as long as the Sisters remained in East Grinstead with the last, that of Sister Eleanor, happening in 2007'. Though the Pieta survives *in situ* the ranks of headstones in 'God's Acre' have since been removed. The bodies have not been disturbed.

Nursing and mission work

The East Grinstead Sisters played an important part in the nursing reform movement spearheaded by Florence Nightingale in the 1850s. The calibre of women attracted to St Margaret's is evident from the following quote by John Mason Neale about Sister Ellen, the first to undertake her training:

> She has just left the Westminster Hospital with the very highest character [reference] from the medical men. She has been in sole charge of three wards, with nurses under her, for three weeks in the absence of one of their Sisters.[139]

It was Sister Ellen who went out on the first call, made to the Sisters from a clergyman in Shoreham where several sick people had been quarantined together in the church school. To get there she took the first ever train to leave East Grinstead station on 9 July 1855.

Earlier that year Neale had set out the terms upon which his nurses would be engaged. Applications from within a twenty-five mile radius of East Grinstead were to be made by parish clergy to the Mother Superior. These were to state the purpose and length of time

Figure 80 *Sr Ellen was the first to receive formal training as a nurse, going on her first mission to Shoreham in July 1855.*

for which the Sister was needed as well as her intended lodging place. If the case was accepted, a Sister would be sent to the applying clergyman for further directions; he would thereafter be responsible for her safety and civil treatment. These last conditions were a recognition of the prejudice that nuns faced. Indeed there were several cases where Sisters arrived only to be sent away again by parishioners who feared their motivations and religious ideology. As to lodgings, the Pulborough vicar who hired a bright yellow gipsy caravan for a Sister called to nurse a family with diphtheria was a unique case. The norm saw Sisters putting up with 'accommodation which a well-cared-for pig would have regarded as totally inadequate.'[140]

Neale specified a geographical limit because he had identified local conditions as particularly problematic:

> There are some parts of England where the poor especially suffer from fever. The low, marshy, unwholesome valleys of the Rother and the Eden, in Kent, are two of them. The Sisters were frequently called to work under such circumstances. Sometimes it was the mother of a family who had nursed

her daughters through the fever, and was herself seized the last; sometimes to a lone woman helpless in her sorrow; sometimes to a widower with his motherless children all laid low together; and then, once, the Sister who nursed such an one and his little children, amid the raving delirium of death, and the intense dread of infection which pervaded the neighbours, lived, day by day and night by night, in the same wretched hovel, a mere lean-to to the actual house, in the midst of a flooded swamp. Surely this was real service to CHRIST, sustained by the strength of His abiding love and power, or else impossible.[141]

As requests for help increased, however, it became clear that theirs was to be a nationwide mission. Around the country, they took on patients that paid nurses refused to attend and in the first ten years dealt with some 420 cases.[142]

During epidemics the Sisters often took charge of whole communities. In 1863 they nursed seventy cases of scarlet fever at Caistor and fifty at nearby Searby in Lincolnshire. The next year they dealt with simultaneous scarlet fever outbreaks in the Hertfordshire towns of Baldock and Hitchin. At Baldock Sister Miriam nursed 140 patients. In the fortnight before she arrived weekly death tolls were twenty and eighteen; after she took over they fell to eight, then four, then two. Neale briefly visited the town and wrote that 'it was like a city of the Plague.' In March 1865 a request came from Aldershot army camp for a Sister to take charge of a temporary scarlet fever hospital; 'she has the rank and rations of a lieutenant, an orderly fatigue party, and the other nurses are absolutely under her.'[143] Sisters also went to Merthyr Tydfil during a smallpox epidemic in 1869 and, for two years from 1871, they ran a smallpox hospital at Hampstead with up to 600 patients in their care at one time. Eighteen years after they were chased out of Lewes, the Sisters nursed an epidemic of typhoid in the town; of the eighty five cases they dealt with, they recorded just eight deaths. Perhaps the most remarkable thing in each instance is how, with just one or two properly trained nurses, they were able to make such a compelling difference to the number of lives lost.

Figure 81 *The striking gables of the Sisters accommodation as viewed from the quadrangle. Each sleeping cell had its own window and was accessed off a rear corridor.*

As cottage hospitals spread and the registration of nurses began, the imperative for the Sisters to follow the path they had initiated was reduced. Nonetheless, their nursing activities for 1887 saw them attending patients in:

East Grinstead, Limpsfield, Bognor, Godstone, Cardiff, Ormskirk, Maida Hill, Fletching, Marlborough, Amblecote, Chiddingstone, Ely, Bath, Forest Row, Alverstoke, Withyam, Wednesbury, Ventnor, Alcester, Windsor, St Leonards, Hartfield, Hordle, Freshwater, Heathfield, Littlehampton, Cobham, London, Newbury, Norwood, Hurstpierpoint, Uppingham, Hever, Blindley Heath, St Ives, Shoreham, Lindfield, Horsham, Clapham, Lingfield, Henfield, Clevedon, Hayward's Heath, Grange Road, Rougheyhurst, Crawley, Swanage,

Lichfield, Lambeth, Pixton Hill, Uckfield, Hever, Groombridge, St Alban's.[144]

Preference was always given to the poor although Sisters did also nurse among the families of their aristocratic patrons. It became rather fashionable to have an East Grinstead nurse and payment for this work helped subsidise their core activities. Surviving notebooks reveal that they were willing to take on all forms of illness as in "The Honble... April 21st – May 5th. Hysteria." or "Mrs... Great Malvern. Jan 17th – 31st. Mental derangement." Care-giving was an essential part of their job, which meant sitting with and reading to patients as well as tending to their medical needs, whatever their social status. If there was a Sister available they were also prepared to travel to English people taken ill abroad and nursed as far away as Odessa, Boulogne, Salzburg and Versailles.[145]

Nursing Sisters returning to the convent welcomed its peace and calm but this did not mean that medical cases were absent from the Mother House. As the community grew and the first generation of Sisters aged, the need for on-site care increased. Sick people also continued to come to the doors of the convent, where

Figure 82 *The infirmary was completed in the same year as the chapel. The design includes a large sculpted cross in the gable and a pair of tiny windows that break the otherwise symmetrical entrance facade.*

the Sister in charge of the lodge performed an important role in assessing them. Prior to the infirmary opening in 1883, cases within the community had to be accommodated in existing buildings. When scarlet fever came to the convent in spring 1875 the embroidery workroom was rapidly converted into a sick bay. Responsibility for nursing the twenty three patients was given to Sister Ermenild (formerly

Figure 83 *Mother Ermenild standing by the entrance to the quadrangle. Born Katherine Ermenild she was the third daughter of John Mason Neale and was elected Superior in 1902.*

Katherine Ermenild Neale, the youngest daughter of the Founder) who took charge on the day after her clothing as a novice on 24 April. By 31 May all her patients had recovered. Other makeshift arrangements were also devised, as in 1880 when young Nelly Willet contracted typhoid and was moved into the guest room. Three days later Sister Elsa also became ill so the two patients were moved into the Mother's room while the Mother decamped to the guest room. There was even an amputation at the convent when Sister Maria had her leg removed by four visiting surgeons in July 1879. It is a relief to note that they also brought their own assistant to administer the ether.[146]

By the time Sister Ermenild was unanimously elected Mother in August 1902 cottage nursing had ceased to be as important as mission work and education. The infirmary was utilised as necessary but quickly had to be brought up to modern hospital standards after Mother Ermenild offered it to the Red Cross when war broke out in 1914. An urgent telegram of 27 August requesting its use for Belgian refugees required the infirmary to be hastily re-adapted but in the end the Belgians were sent to Roman Catholic Communities. Then, at 7pm on 10 September, a policeman and billeting officer arrived to ask how many soldiers the convent could accommodate. Under normal circumstances the infirmary held fifteen patients; the billeting officer assessed it as large enough for 150 men. The Sisters managed to squeeze in eighty or ninety with the residue in the school gymnasium, laundry and St John's House. 'One can picture Mother Ermenild', wrote Sister Gabriel, 'calmly and humorously dealing with the changing situations and being ready for anything.' Though Ermenild was just sixteen when her father died she apparently inherited many of his traits: 'the total absence of any affectation, the tremendous care for every individual, the humour, vigour and deep affection'.[147]

The community did what it could for the war effort though complying with tighter black-out regulations in 1916 proved somewhat troublesome because, as the *Half-yearly Chronicle* informed readers:

> When Mr. Street designed the various shaped windows of the house, he little thought of the trouble which it would give to keep out all chinks of light! The Refectory was the greatest difficulty, as the west window is so high and wide, by the assistance of brown paper, which is stuck over the highest part, and of pulleys which draw up the enormous curtain, this difficulty was overcome.[148]

The Second World War touched the convent more directly since East Grinstead parish church was used as a guide for enemy planes on their flight-path to London and bombs were dropped on the town as they passed over. Raids began in June 1941 when the convent diary records 'Bombs dropped between Forest Row and Hartfield at 3am. The noise woke most of us.' All bell ringing was stopped by government order so the convent was unusually quiet during the day; night time silence was fractured by bomb warnings that kept everyone on the alert. Sometimes the Sisters and orphanage children slept sheltered together in the corridors. By the end of the summer the warnings were sounding day and night. On 14 September there was a 'Fierce battle over E.G. about 10am – 3 German planes were brought down…Bullets picked up in the garden and quadrangle. Very unquiet night.'[149] Many of the boarding school children were evacuated away from southern England so the rooms they left vacant were handed over to Queen Victoria Hospital for the accommodation of airmen and burns victims undergoing the pioneering plastic surgery of Archibald McIndoe. Nursing staff were also lodged in the convent.

The way in which St Margaret's opened up to outsiders is yet another example of the convent's vital place within East Grinstead life although, as should be clear by now, the Sisters could never have been accused of insularity. At any given time there were members of the order doing mission work throughout Britain and the world. This began in November 1858 when Neale's friend and staunch supporter John Charles Chambers, asked for two Sisters to work with him in the parish of St Mary's, Soho. One of those

Figure 84 *Girls from St Margaret's Orphanage represented the convent at key town events including the 1919 Peace Day procession seen here.*

sent to Crown Street was Sister Kate who vividly describes the terrible conditions and wonderful characters she met with there in her *Memoir*. It is clear the mission was life-changing for the people it helped, providing schools to educate around 500 children, a small library, a girls Guild of St Michael and even a drum and fife band for church boys, not to mention the work it undertook visiting the poor and sick. Almost the first mission to open in central London it operated for seven years before transferring to Haggerston where it became an independent daughter house. This followed establishment of the first Affiliated House at Aberdeen in 1864, bound to East Grinstead by the same Rule but run by its own Superior, who was sent from St Margaret's with a group of Sisters the previous year. Again, the initiative came from a friend of Neale's, the Rev John Comper.

Mission work was always undertaken at the behest of a local clergyman and tended to operate only as long as he stayed within the parish or maintained an interest. As a result its duration varied. Early missions included that established at Ash near the military camp at Aldershot to 'help the most fallen of the fallen women of London [who] find their way there…', at Wigan, Frome, Tunbridge Wells, Hitchin, Cardiff and Merthyr Tydfil. From 1888 this work was assisted by the St Margaret's Needlework Society, a national network of highly organised women who ran work parties to make clothes. Each member pledged to sew at least three garments a year; thanks to them the Society was able to give out around 3,000 items of clothing annually.[150]

The range of community works and parish missions peaked under Mother Ermenild so that in 1906 Wallace H. Hills was able to state that:

Figure 85 *The east ward of St Joseph's Hospital at St Mary's Convent, Chiswick. Photograph from the St Margaret's Magazine, January 1912.*

There are to-day branch Orphanages in Hitchin, Worcester and Burton-upon-Trent; Missions in Cardiff, Sunderland, Dundee, Newcastle and Chichester; a Home for Consumptives at Ventnor; a Convalescent Home for Ladies at Kingsand; a Cottage Hospital and Nursing Home at Saltash; a Home of Rest at Shincliffe, a Free Home for the Dying at Clapham Common; and a number of branch works in Ceylon and Johannesburg.[151]

A third Affiliated House had been established at Boston, Massachusetts after Mother Alice and Sister Theresa responded to a plea for help in running the newly established Boston Children's

Figure 86 *The entrance to St Margaret's, Colombo, 1907. The location of the mother house at East Grinstead was announced above the gate of the Sri Lankan mission with the emblem of cross and orb above it.*

Hospital in 1871. Though still a novice, Sister Theresa was left on her own for eighteen months and proved such a success that the decision was made to set up an American convent. Sister Theresa returned to East Grinstead to be professed then got back on a boat with the duly commissioned Mother Louisa Mary and Sister Jessie to formally inaugurate the house in 1873. Now an internationally renowned centre for paediatric medicine Boston Children's Hospital 'owes its existence to those three heroic women.' Their example also prompted young American women to join the order leading to the creation of four branch houses in the US, as well as one in Montreal and work in Haiti.[152]

In 1887 three Sisters set out for Colombo in Sri Lanka (then Ceylon) to work with the poor of St Michael's parish. The convent they started had a significant impact through mission and education work with reports of their activities appearing regularly in the community magazine. The Sisterhood is still active there in the twenty-first century. In 1898 Mother Alice also answered the call from an Irish missionary in Johannesburg to help establish some order in the chaos of a city whose population had exploded as a result of the South African mineral revolution. Mother Miriam took charge of establishing a wide range of schools, classes and choirs, that were supported by the local trades-people who had urged the Sisters to come and that continued as far as they could for the duration of the Boer War. St Margaret's continued to have a presence in South Africa until the 1970s.[153]

Back in East Grinstead the parish works begun by John Mason Neale continued well into the twentieth century. The most ardent local worker was Sister Gertrude who was professed in 1866. She started St Michael's Guild for girls on the same principles as that begun by Neale in Soho and for years after was involved with the mothers' meeting and Mothers' Union (the first branch in the diocese), the night school, the 'Saturday afternoon school' and the 'Sunday afternoon boys'. Press cuttings in the archive record numerous flower shows, sales, fetes, suppers, outings and annual services for all of these organisations. As work grew around the country and the convent schools were enlarged focus necessarily moved away from the town. Changing circumstances saw links strengthened again after World War II.

Though there were celebrations for the centenary of St Margaret's in 1955, the huge alteration in women's lives over that period was already beginning to tell in falling recruitment numbers. Whereas spiritual commitment had been combined with a unique career opportunity in Victorian times, by the mid-twentieth century women's options were considerably enlarged and the existing Sisters were ageing. Financial difficulties, caused by Neale's insistence that the Sisterhood not hold vested property, combined with this decreasing pool of Sisters able to work led to the closure of several houses in 1958, some being handed over to other communities. In subsequent years missions in Sri Lanka and South Africa were also wound up. Attention thereafter returned to helping people within the convent's immediate vicinity and did so with considerable success until the Millenium.

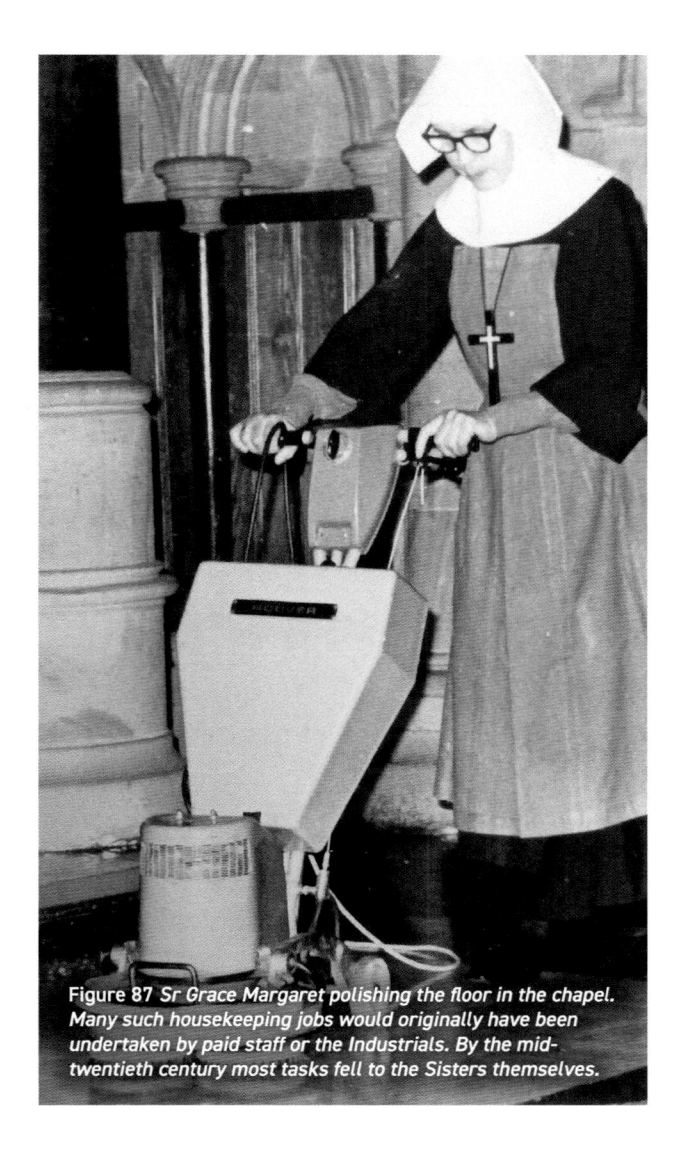

Figure 87 *Sr Grace Margaret polishing the floor in the chapel. Many such housekeeping jobs would originally have been undertaken by paid staff or the Industrials. By the mid-twentieth century most tasks fell to the Sisters themselves.*

Figure 88 *John Mason Neale was the first 19th century Anglican cleric to adopt vestments, which were made and embroidered for him by the Sisters. The cope Neale wears in this portrait was green.*

Ecclesiastical Art

Every well-bred Victorian lady learnt to draw and stitch. John Mason Neale's own artistic sensibilities and search for a decorative expression of his romantic interest in the Middle Ages, meant he actively encouraged the Sisters to pursue these talents, putting them to good use raising funds for nursing and mission work. This was most successful in the field of ecclesiastical embroidery which flourished from the 1850s until 1970 and bought international fame to the East Grinstead Sisterhood.

After the small band of pioneer Sisters moved into their second home on Church Lane in 1858 the most artistic of them worked to decorate the little oratory and brighten the spaces used for the orphanage. On 10 September that year an entry in the community diary records that 'Yesterday Mr Street the architect sent a design for an angel which is to be painted by the Sisters for a new church in Wakefield.' They were also taking orders for illuminated texts, based on medieval manuscripts. These proved so popular during festivals that in Spring 1858 a Sister worked until 4am to finish a commission from Purbrooke Church in Portsmouth. Texts were also undertaken 'illuminated and framed for sitting-rooms'.[154] The first sale of embroidered work mentioned in the diary dates from 24 June 1859 when 'a red [altar] frontal was finished and sent to the Rev. Seymour Walpole of Newark with a white which has also been embroidered by the Sisters.'[155] That the new convent was designed with an embroidery workroom from the outset demonstrates how important this branch of artistic endeavour had already become.

The expanding reach of Oxford Movement ideas led to the construction of new, highly decorative, church buildings where embroidered vestments and altar frontals were crucial to the increased ceremonial of worship. This created a need that had to be supplied and, among the Anglican Sisterhoods who rose to the challenge, St Margaret's established its reputation as one of the best. After the Reformation the wearing of vestments had gradually declined. During the 1830s Pugin was a key figure in their revival, designing new vestments for Roman Catholic churches. He, in turn, influenced the Cambridge Camden Society. Neale wrote about vestments and was reputedly the first to wear them, donning a Gothic style green chasuble with gold-braided orphreys in 1854. It was his architect friends, G E Street and William Butterfield, who took

Figure 89 *Cope made at St Margaret's in 1911 for the Bishop of Chichester as a gift from his Diocese.*

Figure 90 *Sr Isa in the embroidery workroom she made famous. As head of the department her flair for design and commercial acumen led to commissions from around the world.*

over the role of stimulating this embroidery renaissance, inspiring the next generation who took it forward in a more notably Arts and Crafts style. The interpretation of their designs was down to teams of highly skilled embroiderers like those at St Margarets.

The Sisters began by making embroideries for their own oratory but Neale's promotion of his community, as mentioned on page 90, meant that their skill soon inspired commissions from elsewhere. On Easter Day 1862 Neale wore a new white cope made by the Sisters; that summer they finished a banner for the bishop of Honolulu. People travelled to East Grinstead specifically to see the embroidery workroom which, by May 1865, supported four live-in pupils, assisted by local day workers. The following year it became a stand-alone department of the community, on a par with the orphanage and St Agnes' school. Several Sisters were allocated to it, training pupils at the same time as extending their own techniques. Though male designers often worked with the Sisters it is clear this cannot always have been the case and the women's own creativity was highly valued. Trips abroad provided them with new ideas as in 1864 when Miss Townsend (later Sister Zillah) took Sister Alice and Sister Mary to see some of the finest churches and convents in France.

Arguably the most talented figure in the workroom was Sister Isa who was received as a novice in 1861. She had discovered St Margaret's through her brothers, Edmund and John Dando Sedding, both of whom trained as architects in the office of G E Street. In their spare time they used their considerable artistic and musical abilities to brighten the mission of St Mary's, Soho. They urged their sister to come along and Mother Kate, who was the same age as Isabella, remembered her first visit to the mission 'a quiet, gentle girl, with earnest dark grey eyes, out of whose steadfast depths the fire of the Sedding genius flashed.' Isabella's preference for country life drew her to East Grinstead where her sympathetic nature made her a much-loved nurse. It was her artistic flair, however, that made her indispensable. Mother Kate wrote how, through her brothers, Sister Isa came in contact

> ...with members of the Morris and Rossetti school. [William] Morris himself she often met at her brother's home, and so it was that she carried the spirit and glamour of that school of Renaissance down and into the quiet convent workroom, where it permeated all the beautiful embroidery which emanated from her hands.[156]

Sister Isa took charge of the workroom and it was her brothers who designed the two banners carried in the first St Margaret's Day procession of 1865 and all processions thereafter. Four years later the Sisters worked the stunning altar frontal designed by John Sedding for York Minster (fig 69)

As the first convent buildings neared completion in 1870 Sister Isa and her team set about creating the embroideries for their new chapel, temporarily housed in the refectory. Though the ten-foot altar remained unfinished, every effort was made to ensure the altar frontal was ready for opening day.

> So closely were the Sisters run, that the elaborately embroidered frontal, and the vestments worn on St. Margaret's Day by the Celebrant, were begun and finished within six weeks. In the centre of this frontal, the material of which is red velvet, is a figure of St. Margaret under a canopy – the sides being each divided into eight small panels, alternately containing conventional lilies, and what by a figure of speech we may perhaps call stars. The chasuble, also of red velvet, has handwork embroidered orphreys representing series of women saints in front and men saints behind, seventeen in all. This vestment was exhibited in the embroidery-room after the

> service, and attracted much notice from the delicacy of the work and the rapidity with which it was perforce executed. The figure-work of the St. Margaret's embroidery Sisters is the best of its kind which we have seen...[157]

According to embroidery expert Mary Schoeser, the altar frontal is the only known design by G E Street to incorporate figure work. It was made using silk floss, gold and silver passing, silver and silk twist and concavegold spangles. Figure 93 shows how it looked in situ. Its rich red background has faded over time but it does survive, now held in the collection of Liverpool Cathedral's Embroidery Museum.[158]

With completion of the convent's purpose-built workroom in 1871 Sister Isa had a proper space in which to expand. At last there was adequate room for the large frames needed to work altar frontals as well as an upper floor with sleeping cubicles for girls in the training school. Their education included drawing because the St Margaret's embroideries were worked freehand, not from a pattern, and therefore required considerable artistic judgement as well as technical skill. This was no amateur cottage industry. Sister Isa's job involved correspondence with customers, ordering

Figure 91 *The embroidery workroom today. This building was among the first to be completed due to the need for more space to fulfil orders and take on more trainees, who slept in the attic.*

materials, creating designs and then explaining them to her Sister helpers and working girls. For all that the items and the profits they raised were dedicated to the Glory of God, Sister Isa was running a commercial business, managing both accounts and employees, often away

Figure 92 *Detail of the altar frontal designed by Street and made, in great haste, for the opening of the convent in 1870.*

travelling in the company of Mary Arrowsmith, one of the main embroiderers. Work from St Margaret's was shown at the annual Church Congress Meetings and in 1876 at the Centennial International Exhibition at Philadelphia, the first World's Fair held in the US. An entry from the convent diary in 1886 shows Sister Isa going to London to visit both Bodley and Street to select designs for vestments ordered by the Guild of St Alban. As Schoeser observed, 'she was an arbiter of taste, respected by her male contemporaries.'[159] The Sisters also apparently worked designs made by Geoffrey Webb, the stained glass artist resident in East Grinstead High Street from 1914.[160]

In 1870 a second embroidery school was established in London. Known as St Katherine's it was started at 32 Queen Square in Bloomsbury and within five years had been enlarged to take in the neighbouring property. Queen Square was then establishing itself as a centre for the education and professional training of women, not to mention the Arts and Crafts Movement. From 1867-81 Morris & Company had its headquarters a few doors down from the Sisters at number 26 Queen Square. Potential clients found the ground-floor showroom at St Katherine's easier to visit than East Grinstead but work from both places was exhibited there. The school itself operated on two levels, offering the chance for young women to learn a trade whilst also providing instruction to well-off ladies who wished to improve their skills. In 1887 the *Half-Yearly Chronicle* reported that there were twenty working girls in the house, supplemented by ten to twelve outsiders,

Figure 93 *This early photograph shows the frontal at Figure 92 in situ on the altar in the refectory before the chapel was built.*

'chiefly ladies, who eke out their scanty incomes by embroidering.' For the young women starting out, the school offered real hope of a better life as the most skilled embroiderers might go on to earn as much as £50 a year.[161]

The reputation of St Margaret's embroidery schools reached so far that an American article of November 1881 identified them as first of 'the two most famous schools of church embroidery [in England]…' In evidence the author cited the magnificent

> …chasuble of the Rev. Thos. McK. Brown of the church of St Mary the Virgin in this city [New York], worked by the Sisters of St Margaret, London, at what is known as the East Grinstead Embroidery School. This vestment is of white brocaded silk, with a cross on the back whose central ornament is the Virgin and Child, copied from the Sistine Madonna. The arms and body of the cross as well as the front of the chasuble, are enriched with copies of Fra Angelico's angels in embroidery, separated by the Gothic rose in blues and olives. These are on gold cloth, and this mass of gold and colour is applied on the silk with a couching of blue, which frames the cross against the white vestment and completes one of the finest specimens of embroidery in this country.[162]

In 1887 the big commission was an altar frontal for St Paul's Cathedral, designed by John Medland, another former pupil of George Gilbert Scott. It was illustrated in the *Builder* and the *Art Journal* and remained an exemplar of fine raised-gold work well into the 1920s.

Sister Winifred, the first Sister-in-Charge at Queen Square, was a highly talented needlewoman, so much so that her 1879 obituary in the *Church Times* stated that the beautiful embroideries produced under her direction decked the altars of numerous cathedrals.[163] She also cleverly devised a way of baking communion wafers for commercial sale and at one time supplied 1,200 churches. An advertisement from December 1869 offered them plain or stamped with ecclesiastical devices, available in sheets or cut ready for use. Customers were directed to apply to the Rev Mother at East Grinstead or to one of two agents in London.[164]

Wafer baking continued at St Katherine's until the Sisters there separated from East Grinstead in 1902, finally going over to Rome in 1908. The machines were sent to the convent in order to maintain an important income stream but this was not without problem. Space had to be found

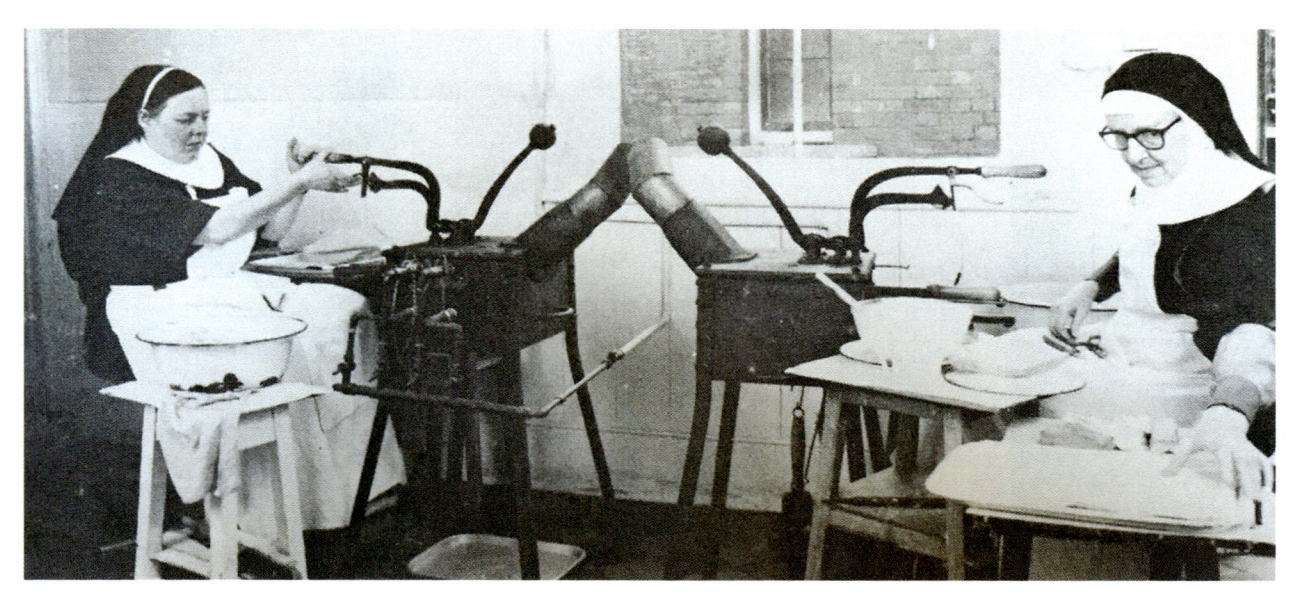

Figure 94 *The Altar Bread department in St John's House, 1970s. Susan Kelland, who was brought up at the orphanage from 1952-62, recalled the girls sometimes having rejected communion wafers as a breakfast cereal affectionately known as 'St Margaret's flakes'.*

for them and the altar breads had to be baked daily to keep up with orders. The Sisters put out an appeal to their Associates and supporters for help: 'It is not everyone who can bake, but what is called "stamping out" is comparatively easy, only it takes time and this second industry will soon employ two Sisters or workers constantly.' Several Sisters were by now 'incapacitated by sickness or advancing years' and the embroidery orders previously fulfilled by London now also required two extra pairs of hands to be kept permanently at home.[165] Somehow they managed and after the St Agnes' girls moved into their new extension in 1908 the wafer bakery was transferred to less cramped conditions in the house known as St John's (see p 162). Mother Gabriel noted that it 'is very much a home industry for all suggestions for enlarging trade by mass-production have been resisted. It is work which provides excellent opportunities for friendship and prayer partnerships.' It was only finally given up in 1981.[166]

Redecoration of the embroidery workroom in 1911 revealed faulty construction in the sitting-room chimney which could easily have caused a serious fire. Whilst this was being remedied a second staircase was added to the building to provide an escape route onto the neighbouring drying ground. The new door and window thus installed helped improve light and ventilation at a very busy phase of the building's existence. That year saw interesting commissions from South Africa, America and Scotland as well as the cope and mitre for the Bishop of Chichester which were to be the gift from his diocese to commemorate the Coronation year. 'And that brings us to *the* event in our history...' – the working of the heraldic embroidery of the Royal Arms for the backs of the Chairs of Estate used by Queen Mary and King George during the early part of the Coronation ceremony in Westminster Abbey. Demanding the highest skill, this bullion work was subcontracted to the Sisters from Morris of Oxford Street, formerly Morris & Company. The chairs were designed after seventeenth century models at Knole Park, whose original velvet fabric was faithfully reproduced. It was a happy coincidence that this pattern onto which the Sisters stitched was named 'Sackville' after the owners of Knole whose support for John Mason Neale allowed the foundation of St Margaret's. The chairs were

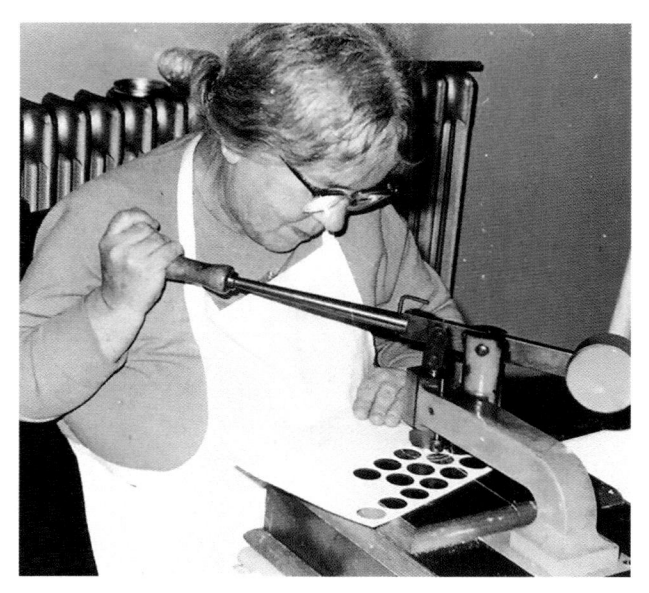

Figure 95 *Miss Nellie Chantler stamping out wafers. The same equipment was used for nearly a century but the sisters resisted calls to modernise because hand production offered time for contemplation.*

shown in several illustrated papers and, after the Coronation, were destined for the Throne Room of Buckingham Palace. Whether or not this job contributed to the number of commissions the Sisters subsequently received is hard to say but between July and December 1912 they completed 100 items of embroidery, sent as far afield as St John's Barbados and New York Cathedral. Closer to home they made an altar frontal for All Saints Church, Crawley Down and a new frontal as well as new curtains for Sackville College.[168]

Figure 96 *Embroidered vestments on display in the refectory for the 1959 Exhibition of Ecclesiastical Art held to raise funds for the Society's global mission.*

Every St Margaret's Day celebration, the embroidery workroom was opened up to visitors for the sale of work to benefit the orphanage. In the early 1900s Sister Edith, carver of the chapel miserere, contributed carvings, inlaid tables and 'specimens of English marquetry'.[169] A more formal exhibition of the community's creative endeavours took place in November 1959 when the refectory was temporarily turned into a gallery to showcase ancient and modern treasures on loan from parish churches throughout Sussex. On the esteemed list of patrons were the Bishop of Chichester, Lady Dorothy Macmillan, Countess De la Warr, Princess Ileana of Rumania and Mr John Betjeman. With the goal of raising much-needed funds for St Margaret's world-wide mission work, some 321 exhibits were gathered together, encompassing church plate, paintings, metal work, stained glass, manuscripts, embroidery and vestments. In view of the Sisters reputation for artistic endeavours it was a highly appropriate place for such an exhibition. Little more than a decade later, however, the famous East Grinstead School of Embroidery was to cease work; the pioneers were long gone and demand had fallen. It remains to be properly acknowledged for the centre of women's art that it was.

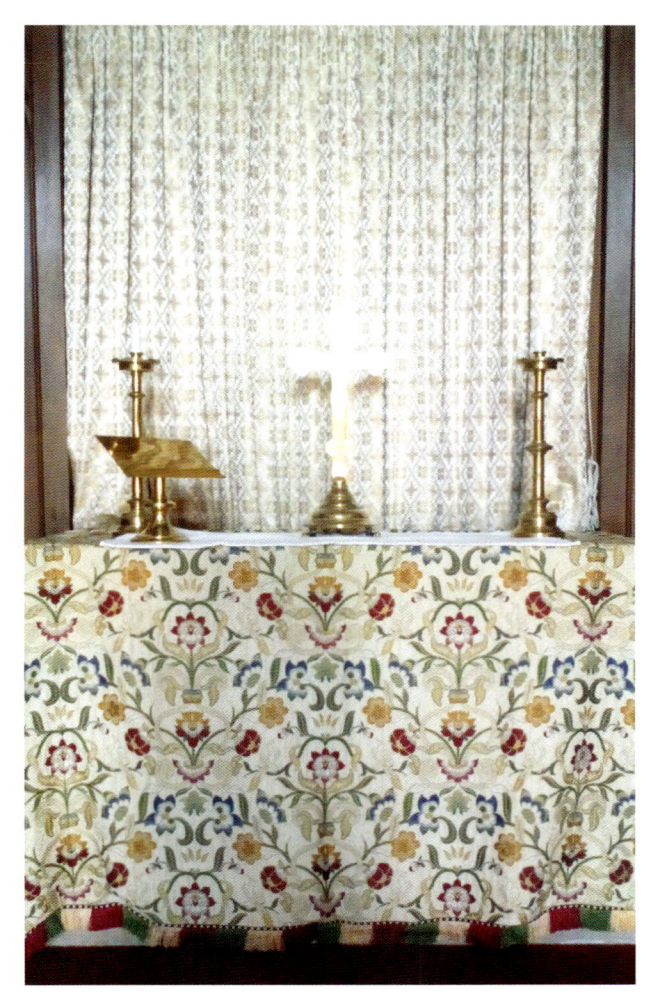

Figure 97 *Long after John Mason Neale's death the sisters continued to make embroideries for Sackville College. This frontal is on display in the chapel where it can be seen by visitors today.*

Figure 98 *Storytelling in the orphanage, 1946.*

Chapter 5
The Orphanage and Schools

St Margaret's Orphanage and the Industrials

In 1857 nine children were transferred to East Grinstead from Elizabeth Neale's orphanage in the Tractarian parish of St Paul's, Brighton. A small brick house was rented for them on the London Road, at the far edge of town, with a fruit garden to one side and a little paddock to the other. Mother Ann put two Sisters in charge and Neale made frequent visits. He catechized the children on Sundays and told them the stories which were subsequently compiled into his book *Sunday Afternoons at an Orphanage.* When teachers were lacking he gave tuition in maths and geography.[170] As a father himself, he took his responsibility for the orphans personally, insisting that they always be clean and well-presented, but also giving them a good deal of attention and special treats. In 1858, after the Sisters moved to No. 1 Church Lane the orphanage found a new home at a neighbouring property becoming a fully integrated part of the community. By 1860 the children numbered twenty-five, their accommodation now spreading across the three terraced houses of 73-77 High Street. Party walls were knocked through at the upper level to create a continuous dormitory while, at street level, a wooden cloister was built to connect the entrances and keep the orphans safe from passing traffic.[171]

The orphanage had its own schoolroom where the best students were awarded copies of Neale's books as prizes in the yearly examinations. There was also a playground after Neale found a nearby field and equipped it with a swing and 'a grand slide.' When exciting events happened he invited the children to Sackville College to share them. In one instance, they all stood in the college field to gaze at a passing comet; another time Neale invited a troupe of visiting circus elephants to meet the children. He took them up the church tower to watch the annual November bonfire, gave them cake and wine for singing to him on his birthday and at Christmas provided a magic lantern slide show with refreshments. Sisterhood diaries record a picnic to nearby Brambletye and an Easter walk to Worth Church from which the children returned with Lent lilies.

There were also trips further afield. On one occasion Neale took three orphans to hear him preach at All Saint's, Margaret Street in London; afterwards they went to the Zoological Gardens. In 1862 Sister Jane and twenty children visited London to see the International Exhibition. The same year Mother Ann took Lizzie, Janey and Marie to Brighton where they went to Holy Communion and Vespers then on

Figure 99 *Sisters and orphans by the cloister in the 1890s. The 'cap girl' (far right) had probably grown up in the orphanage herself and as a teenager took on the care of a small group of younger children in the dormitories.*

to the pier. Among the most memorable trips must have been the grand outing of 4 August 1864 when a large party comprising orphans, the Neale family and nine Sisters set out for the Crystal Palace at Sydenham. There they were met by Sister Mary and Sister Kate from the Soho mission. It was a joyful day rounded off by the novelty of singing Vespers on the station platform while waiting for the train. To keep up the normal routine Compline was sung on the train itself. They returned to East Grinstead at 9.20pm.[172]

Figure 100 *Orphans lined up ready to process out of chapel. The older girls at the rear carry prayer books.*

Such a list of extracted occasions obviously does not reflect the day to day reality of orphanage life but the deprivations suffered by these children meant treats, and the anticipation of them, were extremely important. John Mason Neale was a beloved father figure to the orphans and though his loss was keenly felt the Sisters and their subsequent chaplains kept up his tradition of walks, picnics and outings. Funds to keep the children came from donations so theirs was necessarily a spartan existence but St Margaret's Orphanage was a far kinder place than any Dickensian institution and a world away from the workhouse.

Not all the children were orphans in the modern sense of being parent-less but they came from homes where there was no-one able to look after them. The two cases highlighted in the first issue of the *St Margaret's Magazine,* published in 1887, were sadly typical. Both came from one of London's 'most wretched slums' near St. Thomas', Regent Street. George Thomas had arrived at St Margaret's two years earlier:

> He was pitiful to behold. His poor little legs were scarcely thicker than your thumb. His mother was dead and the rest of his family showed entire indifference towards him.

> He very soon began to thrive and ingratiated himself so much with his hostesses, that they have kept him ever since. Meanwhile his father is dead, his eldest sister has taken to evil courses and his little brother and crippled little sister are gone to the workhouse.[173]

As this example shows, young boys were as welcome as girls. They were kept until the age of five or six when, with hugely improved life chances, they were found places in sympathetic boys' schools.

There was no lower age limit to the children rescued by St Margaret's although the very youngest had to be placed with foster carers in East Grinstead until they were big enough to join the nursery. One such was Susie, a girl of about a year and a half:

> [Her] father, a respectable labourer, died before her birth from the results of an accident; the mother, who had married at sixteen, and was then two-and-twenty, had two or three other children, one taken care of by her own mother, one in the workhouse. She has since disappeared altogether.[174]

Figure 101 *A 19th century studio portrait of three orphans. This may have been taken for fundraising purposes but could also have been intended for family members.*

A wet nurse was found for Susie in the town and paid for by donations but her place in the orphanage the following spring remained subject to funding. The 'Margaret cot' was an initiative to help in this sort of situation. Associates and friends around the world were asked to contribute 10s. 6d. to 'Dolly's Bag' with the goal of raising the £250 needed to endow a free bed in the orphanage. This collecting bag was named after an orphan called Dolly 'Not because she is particularly good or particularly anything, only that she is one of those that belong quite to St. Margaret's.' Twelve years earlier, her father, a London carman, had taken her to one of the

Society's branch houses. His wife had just died of consumption and he did not know what to do with the baby. The Sister-in-charge promised to write to the Orphanage but he set out for East Grinstead and arrived before her letter. 'Of course, a cold wet bundle of humanity, weighing only six pounds, aged three months, could not be refused shelter, at least for one night. Here Dolly has remained ever since…Her father died very soon after, also of consumption, and she has no relations.' St Margaret's orphanage was the only home she knew.[175]

By the time Dolly arrived the orphanage was well established in its final home on Moat Road. Of necessity, it formed part of the first phase, the children moving into the northern range of convent buildings during the summer of 1870. There are few descriptions of this building but in her autobiography Sylvia Spencer recalled growing up there in the 1920s. Though her parents were well-born (her paternal uncle was the painter Stanley Spencer and her Godfather was John Mason Neale's grandson) they had no money and her father's job as an actor meant

Figure 102 *The west front of the convent showing the orphanage building at the northern end nearest the camera.*

Figure 103 *Inside St Dominic's dormitory. This was a typical arrangement of beds and the orphans themselves were responsible for keeping their quarters clean and tidy. All the departments and dorms were named after saints.*

Figure 104 *The orphanage playground. Everyone is assembled and rocking horses have been brought out so this was probably a special occasion.*

their lifestyle was an itinerant one. Sylvia was deposited at St Margaret's without explanation aged about three and half. The room layout and routines she describes can have changed little over those first fifty years. The girls slept in dormitories below the steeply sloping roof, light filtering in from dormer windows with latticed panes. In the nursery on the left side of the passage there were railed cots; on her first night Sylvia was put in the room opposite. There she found rows of iron bedsteads down three sides and the middle. Along the fourth side were enamel washing bowls, pails, jugs and chamber pots. Near the door was a bed reserved for the 'capgirl' in charge of the dormitory. After the bell woke them each morning it was her job, with the help of another capgirl, to make the youngsters 'clean-looking' as they waited in line to meet her flannel.

At night when the girls undressed they folded their clothes into bedside lockers ready to

Figure 105 *The only known view of the new orphanage school is this one taken to mark its opening in 1902. Situated on Hackenden Lane it is now converted into two homes.*

be worn again next day. The uniform had always been blue and white and that worn by Sylvia consisted of a vest, liberty bodice, combinations, bloomers, flannel petticoat, black knee-length socks or stockings (that they learnt to knit themselves), black garters, blue serge dress with a high bound neck piece called a tick and an unbleached holland pinafore, finished off with black boots. Discipline was strict and the walk to breakfast was made in silence. In pairs they passed along the stone passage, 'past the great front door on the right and into the windowless darker part with its polished stone floor.' They turned right, then left, then through the heavy door into the refectory with its long, bare, scrubbed wood tables. Theoretically the whole convent ate together but Sylvia described it being divided into three by partitions that kept the nuns, the fee-paying St Agnes' girls and the orphans in their own separate spaces.[176]

Figure 106 *Two St Lucy's girls (previously known as Industrials) help Sr Lydia Margaret with food preparation in the postwar convent kitchen.*

On weekdays the girls resumed their pairs after breakfast and went to the school room for lessons. Originally this had been within the orphanage wing but the old school room was turned into a playroom after new Education Department standards required construction of an independent building in 1901. This was paid for by a £500 donation from Mr F C Dobbing of Chislehurst, a stalwart supporter and the Chairman of the Free and Open Church Association. The school room's relatively low cost suggests that the stone was quarried from Hackenden as had been the case for the main convent. A E Street was still convent architect at the time so the design must have been his. Simple though it was, Street did add decorative scrolls to the front and rear elevations of the single volume hall which can still be seen in the converted building (now two residences, The Old Stonehouse and Stone Cottage). After the workmen finished time was allowed for the building to dry out so the first classes took place on Tuesday 29 April 1902 when seventy two children 'were in their desks, silently taking in all the glories of their new surroundings.' The walls were colour washed in buff with a three foot high dado of 'rich dark red paint'. A screen painted the same colour was used to divide the room into infants and girls', with matching red curtains at the windows. New desks and a new piano were also installed.[177] In Sylvia Spencer's time the school room was sub-divided into three and she recalled the route there 'out of the huge door, around the lawn edge through a wooded way, across the [orphanage] playground [and] up a tree-lined path...' At dinner and tea time the children returned the same way, back to the refectory.[178]

By 1891 some 500 children had passed through St Margaret's orphanage; the total for its lifetime must have been approaching three times that. That this was not a higher number is explained by the fact many arrived very young and did not leave until teenage. The 'little orphans' taken on by Mother Ann in 1857 were already reaching fourteen or fifteen years old when the Convent opened. As they were being trained for life outside, learning domestic work, teaching and looking after the small children, they began to be known as the 'Industrials'. The convent diaries record their onward progress, for example, on 7 September 1864 'Sarah Buck goes to work for Mrs Greville Ruddock of Cheyne Row, Chelsea, temporarily to help, as she is entirely without servants.' In October that year the Mother put Mary Jane on a train to Manchester; 'She is to be nursemaid to Mrs. Nicholson, Sister Miriam's sister-in-law.' Between placements the young women were able to return to St Margaret's. One of them, Ada Cordelia Dorning (b1870 in Dorset), chose to stay and was welcomed as novice Sister Ada in 1888; 'we felt so pleased and proud.' Sadly she died on 17 September 1889.[179] When the St Margaret's mission at Frome in Somerset, closed in 1878 the older orphan girls there were transferred to East Grinstead. As time went on girls were accepted solely to be trained for service and their department, known from the 1930s as St Lucy's House, occupied part of the north range of the quadrangle, near to the kitchen and refectory where they worked. Though teenage girls were still being received after World War II, by this time their stay was more about putting troubled young women onto a better path than training them for domestic service jobs which no longer existed. St Lucy's closed in 1956.

Figure 107 *Multiple tall windows let light into the orphanage school room where all the classes were taught together.*

Figure 108 *Miss Card's nursery class in the 1960s. The children no longer wear uniforms and the arrangement of desks is considerably less formal than earlier in the century.*

Old girls from SMO were kept abreast of its progress through the pages of the Sisterhood's bi-annual magazine. Information included examination results, reports of outings and letters received from their contemporaries around the world. The former no doubt helped remind readers of the continuing need for funds but taken as a whole the content suggests a strong and ongoing sense of community which cannot be said for all such institutions. Accounts of old girls increased after the turn of the century, presumably because enough of them had then reached an age to look back on their youth. Two letters were chosen to feature in the January 1903 edition, the first from a nurse who went from SMO to train at University College Hospital and was, at the time of writing, stationed in the Burgher Camp at Vryburg having been in South Africa for much for the Boer War. The other was sent from Macomb, Illinois where the writer was living on a farm. She bemoaned the lack of Bible teaching in the American homes around her saying that

> I am glad I had the privilege of taking Bible lessons every day. I am glad I was brought up at St. Margaret's. I well remember the day I left St. Margaret's – how excited I was; I almost forgot to say good-bye to you. I cannot write on this paper how I appreciate your wonderful love and kindness...[180]

In 1906 the *Half-yearly Chronicle* claimed it had been a record year for visits from old girls who were welcomed back to spend their holidays at the convent, often bringing their families with them. When old girls married they were sent a tea set as wedding present from the orphanage.[181]

The most famous, or infamous, old girl was Winifred Marjorie Williams (1897-1980) who was born in Hastings and lived in the orphanage for five years before being taken in by German relatives at the age of ten. Her adopted father Karl Klindworth was a musician and friend of Richard Wagner. Aged eighteen Winifred married Wagner's son Siegfried and, following his death in 1930, took over the running of the family's Beyreuth Festival. In 1923 she met Adolf Hitler with whom she enjoyed such a close friendship that at one point there were rumours of an impending marriage. Although her disgust for Hitler's treatment of the Jews saw their relationship cool during the war Winifred Wagner remained a significant figure in the German far-right throughout her life.

Back in 1857 the sight of uniformed orphans tramping through East Grinstead had been noteworthy, if not troubling to locals, yet a symbiotic relationship was quickly established between town and orphanage, especially where the care of babies was concerned. In 1911 the orphanage girls held their banner of St Margaret high as they took part in the town procession to mark the coronation of King George IV; 'forward we marched along – cheering all sides of us, soldiers in front of us, schools to the rear of us...' then home for a special tea provided by the East Grinstead Coronation Committee.[182] Between the wars, when Sylvia Spencer lived at SMO, the old ways continued without major upheaval but this could not continue after World War II. It was now very apparent that the girls needed wider and more advanced education than that which could be offered in the small orphanage school room. Arrangements were therefore made to send them to state schools. It was a necessary development but one that, as Sister Gabriel noted, 'changed the nature of the Orphanage completely...it became more like a school hostel, with much less close ties with the [Sisterhood] Community... They were no longer "our" children...'[183]

The Convent Schools – St Agnes', St Margaret's and St Michael's

By the beginning of the twentieth century three separate schools were being run at the convent. The first to be established was the orphanage discussed above, which was followed in 1862 by St Agnes', a boarding school catering for the daughters of wealthy gentlemen. St Margaret's College, created in 1895, provided day and boarding places for middle class girls local to East Grinstead. In 1917 the confusion caused by operating St Margaret's College at St Margaret's Convent, alongside St Margaret's Orphanage, led to a name change and the college became St Michael's. By 1933 the replication of staff and facilities no longer made sense; under Mother Madeleine's leadership the two fee-paying schools were combined into St Agnes' and St Michael's, affectionately known as 'Ag and Micks'. In 1965 orphanage girls who had failed to prosper in the state system were also integrated into the student body. Just over a decade later the changing circumstances of the Sisterhood led to closure of this, the last remaining convent school.

Education emerged as a key strand in the St Margaret's mission from soon after its foundation. Mother Kate recalled that John Mason Neale was 'keenly interested in the bettering of women and girls.'[184] Partly this was tied to a, now very old-fashioned, notion of purity; that is, giving girls the tools to remain unstained by worldliness in order for society to benefit from the civilizing influence of their femininity in the home. It was also clear, however, that Neale had an unusually high regard for women's intellectual abilities. He once set two of the Sisters to translate a text from Flemish even though neither of them knew the language; he simply expected them to learn it.

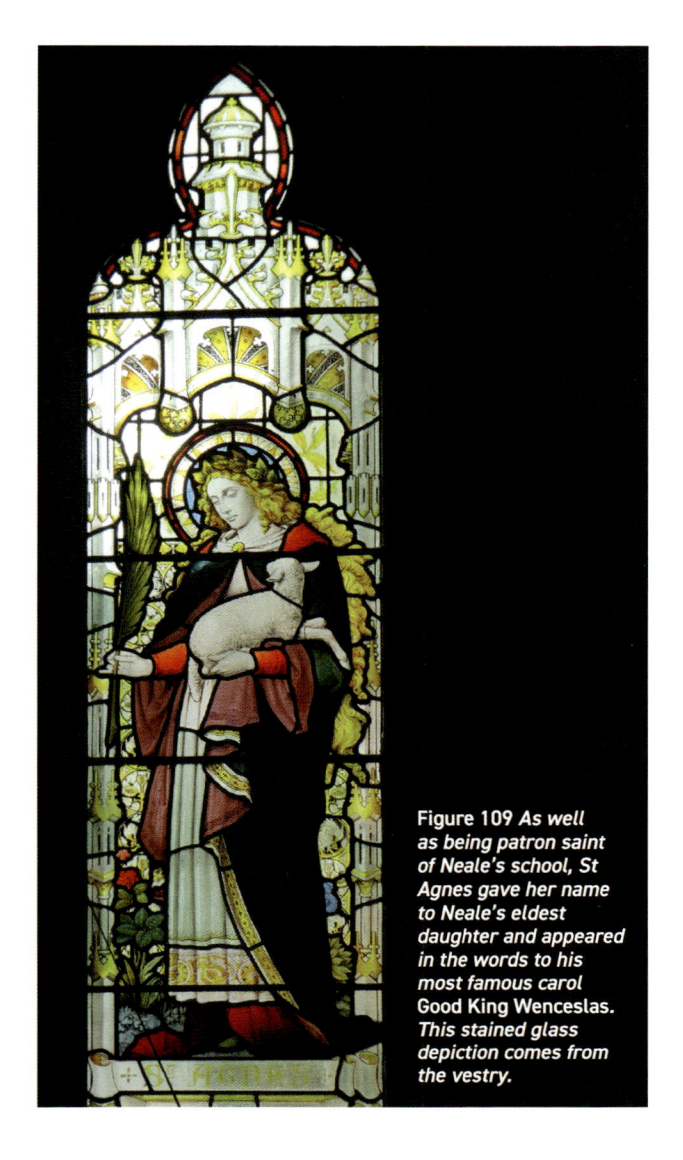

Figure 109 *As well as being patron saint of Neale's school, St Agnes gave her name to Neale's eldest daughter and appeared in the words to his most famous carol Good King Wenceslas. This stained glass depiction comes from the vestry.*

As early as summer 1856 the Sisterhood began teaching the daughters of East Grinstead tradesmen in a schoolroom converted from a detached washhouse at the rear of No. 8 Church Lane. There was a pragmatic reason behind this development for, as Neale wrote in a letter to Benjamin Webb on 10 June, 'we must do everything to make the Sisterhood self-supporting'; running a school was a means toward that end. He had looked into the fees charged by English Roman Catholic Convent schools and found that six guineas was the average. By September Neale's elder daughters, Agnes and Mary, had joined as pupils.[185] Though the fallout from the 1857 Lewes Riots put an end to this school, in November 1858 another was begun. The Red School, so named because the girls were to wear red dresses, had a different purpose being designed 'for girls, not orphans, that can be saved out of such families as would pretty well secure their ruin were they allowed to remain.' Sister Kate looked after the first two pupils rescued from Wapping but the distinction between them and the orphans was so minor and the demands on the Sisterhood so great that the Red School idea floundered.[186]

Experimentation was an essential hallmark of early Anglican Sisterhoods. They came into existence to meet social needs and as the movement towards women's higher education gained pace, they were able to make an important contribution. To pass the university entrance exams girls needed the same level of education as boys; at mid-century few of them got it. Whether placed in the hands of a governess or sent to one of the small private establishments run by spinsters in large houses, the quality of teaching for girls was very hit and miss. New church schools began to provide an alternative, as did convent schools. Along with St Anne's, Rewley House in Oxford and St Stephen's College, Clewer, St Agnes' at East Grinstead was one of the first. By providing education the pioneering generation of Sisters were helping to ensure crucial new opportunities for the young women who followed them.

As far as St Agnes' was concerned, the reminiscences of Sister Miriam (b. Mary Anne Nicholson, 10 Sept 1830) suggest that the impetus came, as it had done for the orphanage, from force of circumstance. In many respects it was a similar undertaking since girls were accepted from a young age and might not leave until they were around seventeen. Though from a more socially elevated position some boarders rarely went home, either because their parents

Figure 110 *Not long after its construction this house on Moat Road was taken over by St Agnes' school. Known as St Cecilia's it would later form part of St Michael's, the second convent school.*

Figure 111 *St Agnes' pupils pose outside their school building in the 1890s. Girls thinking of joining would have been encouraged by the racquets in this image at a time when tennis was the most fashionable new sport among well-bred girls.*

were dead or because they lived elsewhere in the British Empire. Sister Miriam's first work after joining the Sisterhood was in St Agnes', the germ of which she dated to the arrival of a little girl called Charlotte Dinham, sometime in 1861. Charlotte was the daughter of a Cornish doctor who had fallen on hard times. Dr Dinham had been nursed until his death by Sister Ellen who, taking pity on his impoverished widow and family, agreed to take one of the girls back with her to East Grinstead. Being of a different social class to the orphans Charlotte was placed in the care of one of the Sisters in whose room she slept. Although she was also dressed differently to the other children, wearing a large straw hat with long blue ribbons, her days were mostly lived among them in the orphanage. The question of separate accommodation arose when Charlotte was subsequently joined by two sets of sisters, Barbara and Annie Mackenzie from Scotland and Jane and Myra Griffinhoofe. Jane sadly died but the addition of Sister Elizabeth's two elder children and the niece of one of the Sisters working at Wapping, Fanny Thelwall, made seven pupils to start the school. In December 1862 John Mason Neale was able to report that the newly founded St Agnes' 'goes on flourishing.'[187]

Pupils lived in a semi-detached house near the London Road end of Moat Road; 'very small, and very badly built, but I don't think there was much grumbling. The Oratory was at the top; an attic with sloping ceiling on both sides, so that grown people could only stand in the middle.' Luckily most of the congregation were small enough to fit in at the sides. Each day they walked to the Mother House on the other edge of town to attend Vespers and 'the two Sisters in charge took it in turn to go up to the early Mass there.'[188] By the end of 1862 the next-door house was also taken and Neale reported that 'We have five new pupils coming, all well, this Christmas.'[189] Even together the two properties could only accommodate sixteen so, in the same letter that Neale reported on the purchase of the convent site in 1864, he also wrote that Agnes' has marvellously prospered. A large new house we have now, not ugly, on the common. We have thirty-three girls, and are continually having fresh applications.'[190] The new St Agnes' house was detached and in its own grounds further along Moat Road though it too needed to be enlarged after it was 'filled to overflowing'. The neighbouring detached house was rented and named St Cecilia, the two being connected by a covered way.[191]

Between 1865 and 1885 the Sister in Charge was Sister Susannah (Susannah Williamson, d. December 1922) who oversaw the school's move to its purpose-built premises at the convent in 1874.

On G E Street's 1879 perspective view (fig 57) the school range is marked in the foreground, occupying the outward-facing eastern section of the main quadrangle, next to the chapel which was still awaiting construction. Comparison with the 1865 drawing (fig 36) shows how the design had changed from a simple range with three clusters of three chimneys into a more interesting elevation broken by two external chimneys that rise through the wall to punctuate the roof line, giving extra emphasis to the dormer windows, two large and one small. Comprising dormitories and classrooms, it was paid for by two comparative strangers who between them donated £3,000. In 1879 students began to be examined by the Cambridge Syndicate with the brightest girls taking Higher and Matriculation Examinations. In 1903 a representative from the Board of Education recognised St Agnes' as a secondary school but did so only on the understanding that improvements be made to the premises which were by now far too small.

Figure 112 *The St Agnes' dormitories were less spartan than those provided in the orphanage with patterned coverlets and curtains to provide some privacy between beds*

Figure 113 *This 1850s house on the edge of the convent site was known as St John's. Over the years it provided overflow accommodation to the orphanage and schools before becoming home to the wafer bakery.*

By the turn of the century the original schoolroom was having to double-up as a recreation room for junior classes. Two upper forms were being taught in St John's, a house on Moat Road, which was also being used to provide overflow sleeping accommodation. St John's had been acquired by the Sisterhood during the mid-1860s when it provided much-needed extra space for the orphanage. It was named by Mother Alice but Neale, in a reference to the Anti-Confessional disturbances happening in Brighton around 1865, specified it be in homage to St John of Nepomuck, the Saint who suffered death rather than violate the Seal of Confession.[192] It later became the wafer bakery and though the house no longer survives, gave its name to St John's Road.

The need to extend St Agnes' had long been apparent. Mother Alice had asked Arthur Street to prepare plans as early as 1892 and that year an illustration of a grand fireplace intended for the new school assembly room appeared in *The Builder*. Lack of funds precluded these being acted upon and it was a matter of regret to the Mother that she was unable to see this project through. Following her death, a memorial fund was created for the purpose of erecting these buildings. Necessity required that a new lavatory block be built in 1903 and it proved a good thing that the Sisters did not wait to begin this. Three years later the Memorial fund had only achieved one tenth of the £3,000 needed to commence the full extension and, as the *Half-yearly Chronicle* ruefully observed 'at this rate of increase it will be twelve years at least until we can start work.'[193]

By the end of 1906 convent architect Mr Stockdale had prepared plans to be laid before the Local Authorities for approval, Mr Street having retired. The first stone was laid by the Bishop of Chichester on St Margaret's Day 1907 and

Figure 114 *The school badge of the amalgamated St Agnes' and St Michael's, affectionaly known as Ag and Mick's.*

Figure 115 *A new St Agnes' school house was built in 1928. It subsequently became the senior school classrooms. Now called Cricket Court, it is subdivided into three houses.*

work finally got underway. The contractors were Norman and Burt of Burgess Hill who were to be paid £6,275 for completion by 31 May 1908. Although the Sisterhood was still some £5,000 short of the final figure, pressure from the Education Department compelled them into action.[194] There was no intention to raise pupil numbers beyond the usual sixty because neither the chapel nor refectory could hold more. The priority was to upgrade, so the extension had a large assembly room or gymnasium on the ground floor with the rest of the space comprising 'two good class-rooms, five music rooms, dormitories, containing twenty-seven beds, and four bedrooms, besides a good bath-room, box-room and various other offices.'[195] Designed in a rather Arts and Crafts version of Gothic, with a handsome tie-beam roof, it was furnished during the 1908 summer holidays ready for the girls return in September; it was officially blessed on St Agnes' Day 1909.

The normal routines of school life and the religious observance that went with it continued, working towards examinations, dramatic performances and sporting endeavours. An unlooked-for novelty occurred in the summer of 1918, however, when pupils got to experience War work. Male labour shortages meant that the cricket field could not be maintained and was left to grow to hay. At the end of June two Mistresses went with senior girls in their sunbonnets to make said hay. This they did, 'turning, raking in, pitching on to the wagon, and, owing to the difficulty in getting horses, even dragging the cart through three fields to the rick.'[196] By 1924 school facilities were again in need of updating. The plans drawn up by Mr Stockdale for a second extension, to be built onto the 1908 building, survive in the Pusey House archive. These comprised a studio, science room, more class rooms and music rooms, a library and reading room, rooms for the head mistress and teaching staff, plus a well-equipped Kindergarten. The projected cost was £9,500, an expense that was justified because

> ...additions to George Edmund Street's best conception, as he termed his design for the Neale Memorial, cannot take shape in ordinary bricks and mortar. The very stones would cry out if the new building did not harmonize to a certain extent with the existing group of gabled roofs and mullioned windows.[197]

This was a remarkably enlightened view to take during the interwar period when Victorian buildings were generally seen as old fashioned. Fundraising proved as slow as ever and despite a legacy in 1927 there was insufficient money to begin work.[198] The need for more space was resolved by the amalgamation of St Agnes' School with St Michael's College in 1933.

When the forerunner to St Michael's was established in 1890 distinctions between social classes were still very much in evidence. St Margaret's day school offered a cheaper education than St Agnes' and drew its catchment from East Grinstead and surrounding area. Like the other two convent schools, it began in a small house. By 1892 it had grown sufficiently to take over one of the detached Moat Road houses formerly occupied by St Agnes'. This property was subsequently extended to designs made by A E Street and became St Margaret's College in 1895. Although boarding places had increased to meet demand there were always more day pupils to keep tuition costs down; in 1895 the £30 annual fees covered lessons in German and Latin, along with book keeping and shorthand to prepare students for work in the expanding clerical sector. This contrasted with the more elite education offered at St Agnes' which cost £50 a year plus extras and included German and Italian, drawing, library privileges and plentiful extra curricular activities.[199]

Over the next two decades St Margaret's College continued to expand along the Moat Road edge of the convent property. In 1903 the Board of Education made it the only recognised secondary day school for girls in East Grinstead, opening up the possibility of government grants. As at St Agnes', this required significant improvements to the facilities which seem to have been undertaken without recourse to outside fundraising. In 1908 the Convent Trustees bought Oakfield Lodge, a large detached house between the college and St John's that had been empty for two or three years. This was converted into a new refectory and kitchens with the first floor used for staff accommodation and nurseries. Over time the corridor which connected it to the existing

Figure 116 *Though A E Street designed the St Agnes' extension to blend in with his father's complex the detailing of his Edwardian Gothic is rather more frilly in style.*

Figure 117 *Pupils demonstrate the latest exercise equipment of clubs and bars in the new St Agnes' gymnasium.*

Figure 118 *St Margaret's College (later St Michael's) was so successful at educating girls from the professional classes that its premises expanded rapidly along Moat Road.*

buildings was replaced by additional school structures. To the rear were gardens, a tennis lawn and playing fields. After its name change to St Michael's in 1917 the school continued to thrive and by 1925 it had space for 112 pupils.

The merger of St Michael's with St Agnes' in 1933 was part of Mother Madeleine's reforming agenda. Not only had Victorian class distinctions become less relevant, provision for girls education elsewhere had also substantially improved. Joining the two institutions simplified an important part of the Convent's mission. Other modernisations transformed the chapel, the finances, the care of the buildings, and the daily life of the children. As Mother Gabriel noted, her predecessor's endeavours ensured that 'Everyone in the Convent was better warmed, fed and clothed.'[200] All school dormitories were now concentrated in the main G E Street complex with most of the teaching taking place in the buildings along Moat Road. In addition there were new classrooms in a block built next to the orphanage school in 1928 (fig 115). After its use as the senior school classrooms ceased it was converted to residential accommodation. Now called Cricket Court it is accessed off Hackenden Lane where a row of houses once accommodated teaching staff who did not belong to the Sisterhood.

Figure 119 *In the foreground of this 1930s aerial view St John's House can be seen right of the convent entrance road with the school buildings to the left where St Agnes Close is now.*

In 1962 the convent school celebrated a century since the foundation of St Agnes'. Its 320 pupils, of which 140 were boarders, took part in a four-day anniversary festival attended by more than 1,000 visitors. A press report declared that 'this famous Convent School is rich in local history and the daughters of many very well-known families have attended.'[201] Pattie Boyd was only just embarking upon her international modelling career at the time but was to become one of the school's most famous alumni. Mrs Margaret Westall of Stoven in Suffolk represented three generations by her attendance at the centenary; her mother was an Old Girl, as was she, and her two daughters were current pupils. She no doubt took part in the service of Thanksgiving in the convent chapel, marvelled over the photograph gallery that showed the school's development and watched the special performance of Gilbert and Sullivan's 'Iolanthe'. Memories posted on Facebook from Old Girls who attended 'Ag and Micks' suggest it was a happy place to grow up in the 1960s but sadly major change was on the horizon.

Figure 120 *1960s pupils outside the newest Moat Road school building. The Victorian block behind echoes the Queen Anne style of Newnham College, Cambridge where the top girls might go on to study.*

Members of the Sisterhood resident at the Mother House were by now much reduced in number. Staffing levels were also far below what they had been at the turn of the century; one gardener maintained the grounds where there had previously been seven. With the closure of St Lucy's, kitchen and housekeeping tasks previously undertaken by students had to be simplified and redistributed among the Sisters. The formal dining of the past gave way to self-service cafeteria style meals with Sisters doing the clearing and washing up afterwards, albeit in the traditional silence. Then there was the issue of maintenance and repairs to the Victorian buildings which had long been a considerable drain on funds but looked set to increase in the future. 'At length a daring Sister proposed to Chapter

Figure 121 *The 1972 St Margaret's Day procession took place amid building work as the Sister's moved out and the school took over the whole site.*

that we should move out of our beautiful and much loved Convent. The instant furore which followed this suggestion lasted a surprisingly short time, as Sisters reflected upon the hard facts and discussed them together.'[202] The two key questions of what to do with the convent buildings and how to keep St Agnes' and St Michael School going seemed to be answered by a plan that would deal with both.

In 1972 St Agnes' and St Michael merged with a small school previously based at Horley, known as Kingsley, to become the school of Kingsley St Michael. The Kingsley headmistress was to take charge of academic work, the Sisters were to run the boarding and continue their teaching responsibilities and, crucially, the whole of the convent buildings, as well as the existing school premises, were to be turned over to school use. On a single day, in April 1972, the Sisters left for alternative accommodation within the Order and the entire contents of the convent were moved out into allotted rooms and garden sheds to await their installation in a new, lower maintenance convent. This was designed by architect Kenneth Smith and was built in a field alongside the convent gardens, where the pigs had always been kept. Mother Gabriel remained in office to see the new St Margaret's occupied in 1975 then retired the following year, after nearly eighteen years service. Mother Hazel was elected as her replacement in May 1976 and immediately faced the task of having to close the school, 'made even more painful than it would otherwise have been by the fact that she herself had been educated at St Agnes' and later at the School of St Agnes' and St Michael.' [203]

The closure caused anger and frustration for the parents and students of 'Ag and Micks' who saw their previously thriving school irredeemably damaged by its amalgamation with Kingsley. In 1972 St Agnes' and St Michael had 450 pupils to which 100 were added from the Horley campus; within four years the total school population had dwindled to 280. Fees quadrupled to try and meet the shortfall but Kingsley had to come to East Grinstead in the first place because of a sizeable hole in its finances; the sale of its former premises to developers had been required to repay the bank. Parents claimed mismanagement and tried to step in to save the school but the damage was already done.[204] Whereas the unification of three separate convent schools into one had worked because they all shared the same basic culture, emanating from the Sisterhood, the addition of an outside school ultimately failed. It had to be attempted, however, because the ageing demographic of the Sisters and their need to downsize operations meant that St Agnes' and St Michael could not have continued on its established path indefinitely. The closure of the school on 14 July 1976 left the convent buildings redundant.

Thankfully they had been added to the Department of the Environment list of historic buildings at Grade II* on 2 August 1972. This designation recognised the remarkable completeness of Street's original complex; it was revised to Grade I in 1981. Since the St Agnes' extension of 1908 the only addition had been new rooms in the kitchen court for Kingsley St Michael School and these were well tucked away out of sight. As the Victorian Society pointed out 'Practically all of the other large Victorian convents, including Street's earlier one at Wantage, Henry Woodyer's large and forbidding red-brick one at Clewer, and Butterfield's picturesque one at Plymouth, have been seriously altered or overwhelmed by later additions; while many of the smaller ones have been demolished altogether.'[205] With a sympathetic purchaser secured, St Margaret's became one of the first Victorian convents converted for residential use and is now split into thirty one unique homes.

Figure 122 *The 1976 convent by Kenneth Smith was a smaller, simpler structure that nevertheless referenced its predecessor in the saddleback roof of its chapel tower.*

Figure 123 *Street created a dynamic west front with the gables of the kitchen, refectory, chapel and tower jostling for attention.*

Chapter 6
Change and Legacy

In 1976 Moor House Estates bought the Old Convent and secured listed building consent for its subdivision. A legal covenant of the sale required that the chapel could only ever be used for cultural or educational purposes but all other spaces were subsequently conveyed to independent purchasers on 999 year leases. From 1978, properties were sold unconverted with new owners completing the necessary building work themselves. The chapel and grounds, including swimming pool, were held in common ownership under the care of The Old Convent Estate Residents Limited (TOCERL), a management company run by residents, which held its first meeting on 15 August 1978. In 2013 TOCERL bought the freehold for £23,000 thereafter leasing the common parts back to itself. It runs a comprehensive programme of annual maintenance which, along with work for individual residents, is sufficient to employ someone full-time. Since 2016 TOCERL has also been responsible for upkeep of the convent cemetery which had been retained in the Sisters' ownership until that time.

Development of the larger convent site took place in phases. The former school buildings along Moat Road were divided in two; those at the southern end were sold off and in March 1980 Ideal New Homes of Woking, Surrey, submitted plans for construction of St Agnes' Road and Mason Close. Moatfield Surgery was built on land purchased from the nuns behind this in 1987. The remaining school buildings, centred around the former Oakfield Lodge, were turned into a conference centre called Neale House. This was run by a Sister-in-Charge with the help of a lay warden and his family. As well as hosting regular weekend residential conferences and retreats, Neale House was used by many local groups including the Camera Club, Literary Society, the Soroptomists and Machine Knitters. Classes in ballet, keep-fit, swimming and Karate were held there as well as a term-time playgroup. The Sisters themselves did valuable parish work at St Swithun's Church and made weekly visits to Sackville College, to the 'Peanut' Children's Ward at Queen Victoria Hospital, and to local people living alone or in residential and nursing homes.

Until the early 1990s there remained a strong sense of continuity within the East Grinstead Sisterhood; several surviving Sisters at that time were still able to recall members of the generation professed in the nineteenth century. Sister Joan Margaret (d 1995) and Sister Mary Joan (d 1998) were themselves professed during

Figure 124 *Drawing of the west entrance gate as it is today by Susan Quekett.*

Saint Margaret's Convent, East Grinstead

PATRONAL FESTIVAL

The Dedication day has been the really great event of this year, but the Mother and Sisters have pleasure in inviting you to join them on

Monday, 21st July 1975   SUNG MASS 11 a.m.

Preacher: **THE BISHOP OF HORSHAM**

Sale of Work.   Please bring a picnic lunch.
Coffee and soft drinks will be provided.

Would you be so kind as to return the enclosed slip if you intend to come, so that we shall have some idea of numbers

---

Figure 125 *Even after the Society left the Old Convent their Patronal Festival remained an important event with locals and supporters invited to enjoy a summer's picnic with the Mother and Sisters.*

Mother Ermenild's period of office, thereby tracing a line back to her father, the Founder. Such links were necessarily diminished by time and it became harder to sustain the community in East Grinstead. St John's House on Moat Road, which since its purchase by John Mason Neale had accommodated orphans, school children, teachers and wafer baking operations, had latterly been used as a guest house where up to a dozen visitors were able to come and share in the Community of St Margaret's worship and find respite from the strains of modern life. A review by the Convent Chapter in 2000 decided, however, that both St John's and Neale House had become too expensive to maintain. The latter was sold and replaced by Meadow Court retirement housing. In 2006 the new convent itself was demolished; flats have since been built on the site. Around G E Street's Old Convent a strip of land remained to give a sense of the original pastoral setting. As the Sisters withdrew from East Grinstead this too was sold. Proposals by Fairview New Homes for 125 dwellings were gradually resolved into a less intensive development and after a lull caused by the 2008 financial crisis the houses of Sister Ann Way were finally built in 2016-17. The effect has been to connect the Old Convent to the wider town in a more obvious way, though it remains a private community.

By this point the Sisters from East Grinstead had moved to other communities within the Order. Until 2015 the Mother House remained in Sussex, at Hooke Hall in Uckfield. For the next four years a small number of Sisters stayed in Uckfield though the Mother House and the majority of their colleagues moved to St Mary's Convent, Chiswick. The successful nursing home they run there first became part of the Community more than a century ago. In addition to this, the Order has autonomous houses at St Saviour's Priory, Haggerston (where Sister Kate, who wrote about her early years at East Grinstead, was first Mother Superior) and at The Priory of Our Lady Walsingham in Norfolk. In November 2019 Sister Alma Mary died at Walsingham aged ninety-one. Born in Trinidad, Sister Alma was professed at East Grinstead in 1960 and was a favourite with pupils at the convent school, with many of whom she kept in touch. Indeed, the continuation of alumni links to 'Ag and Micks' Old Girls remains an important part of the St Margaret's mission.

Elsewhere in the world the Order remains active in America where St Margaret's Convent at Duxbury, Massachusetts also has daughter houses in Boston, New York and Port-au-Prince, Haiti. From St Margaret's Convent at Polwatte in Colombo, Sri Lanka the Sisters run a retreat house, a children's home (mainly for those orphaned in the civil strife), a hostel for young women and a home for elderly people, as well as being involved in parish work and church embroidery.

As the following summary from Sister Sarah shows, the basic Christian mission in all these places is the same as it has always been. Though the children's books and the methods of delivering help to the needy are modern they come from the same place.

> [Is it] A daunting task? Or an exciting challenge? Each of us looking for God's activity in the circumstances of our own lives.... – in the trust and inner search of those who come to talk – in listening to the eight year old stumbling through the dreary doings of Horrid Henry – or in heaving boxes of tins around the Foodbank warehouse or collecting offerings from the supermarket and churches – the Lord is there, in the minutiae of the mundane. It's not so much about understanding as it is to see and believe as the outcome of Job's story – seeking to enable people to see what God has done in His Son Jesus Christ, – seeing

Figure 126 *Continuing their mission wherever they were needed, with the help of the 1970s Convent car.*

Two sisters set off in the Convent car, one for the station, the other on Diocesan work.

that all human activity is somehow bound up and inspired by His life on earth and in heaven, – seeking to show the relevance of worship – praise, thanksgiving, restoration and forgiveness and involvement in the hopes and struggles of humanity.

In her words can be found that sense of vigour Sister Kate wrote of in the 1850s when she and her colleagues were 'all very keen on *doing*... we all hung together, and we all pulled together.'[206]

The legacy of care established by John Mason Neale and the first Sisters of St Margaret is ongoing. In the cause of women's emancipation the hard work was done in days gone by. Historian Susan Mumm has analysed the place of Anglican sisterhoods in Victorian society:

> Their inventive and evolving community structures gave women independence, autonomy and control over their own lives; they provided a nurturing woman-affirming environment while also providing creative, fulfilling work. The work they did became a significant element in the history of Victorian philanthropy, as well as giving the lives of the sisters profound meaning. Both in their convents and in their work, religious communities empowered women. They validated the worth of women, their abilities and their labour, 'in a world that seemed materialistic, godless and male.'[207]

If this were the only way sisterhoods contributed to the growing liberation of women it would be impressive enough. As this book demonstrates, the East Grinstead Sisters were nurses, teachers and social workers before any of those jobs became valid professions for middle and upper class women. And beyond the Sisters themselves, their legacy stretched to the many thousands of girls' lives they enhanced by education, whether it be in the convent schools, orphanages, night schools or guilds.

The architectural manifestation of Neale's aspirations for the Sisterhood also had significant influence. George Edmund Street, who gave his designs for the Old Convent for free, was a key figure in the dissemination of High Victorian Gothic. Though this style changed the parameters of Anglican church building its impact went beyond religious structures. In the particular case of Mr Street, his advocacy of local materials and his ability to create a Victorian blend of foreign and historic Gothic forms, as seen at East Grinstead, was to profoundly affect the direction of men who worked in his office, men who went on to become leaders of the Arts and Crafts Movement. William Morris, Philip Webb and Richard Norman Shaw may or may not have had direct personal experience of working for the Society of St Margaret but they surely knew of their master's designs for the convent. Edmund and John Dando Sedding certainly had a continuing involvement through their siblings, Sister Isa and Sister Christina. These artistic networks fed into the designs produced by the embroidery workroom at East Grinstead. In architectural terms it is interesting to compare the design of the convent with that of nearby Standen built by Philip Webb and now owned by the National Trust. In many ways the latter is a direct descendant of the former. At Standen Webb used the same local sandstone that Street employed at the convent, taking the interplay of

Figure 127 *The garden front of Standen, outside East Grinstead, designed by G E Street's pupil Philip Webb and built 1892-4. A key building in the Arts and Crafts Movement, Standen's gabled elevation references the Sisters' cells at St Margaret's.*

multiple other vernacular materials to the next level of subtle complexity. The ethos of truth to materials that came to underpin the Arts and Crafts Movement is apparent in both buildings, the convent offering an early signpost to the future direction of Victorian architecture.

John Mason Neale's personal legacy has been examined in other books but it is certain that through the Cambridge Camden Society he had a profound impact on how we visualise Victorian churches. As a leading hymnologist he also influenced how churches sound and in the public consciousness he is perhaps best known as the writer of *Good King Wenceslas,* published in 1853 and still in the nation's top thirty favourite Christmas carols, according to a 2019 survey by radio station Classic FM.

Christmas was a very important festival at the convent, full of anticipation and delight for members of its community. An account from the first convent magazine provides an evocative sense of how it was celebrated by Victorian occupants. On Christmas Eve the orphanage schoolroom was decorated and Christmas cards were addressed amid a 'perfectly unceasing chatter of expectation.' The men and boys of

Figure 128 *Giving out presents beneath the massive convent Christmas tree in the 1940s.*

the night school came in to sing carols with the children and the youngest orphans hung up their stockings to be filled by a Sister during the hours of darkness from a 'basketful of treasures, pictures, oranges and goodies.' A few of the older children enjoyed the privilege of staying up for the beautiful midnight service. On Christmas Day there were more choral celebrations before, at dinner time, 'eager faces watch the Sisters carrying in the flaming puddings'. In the refectory the nativity crèche was arranged in the recess formed by the oriel window with a 15ft high Christmas tree next to it, lit by hundreds of tapers and coloured glass lanterns. After guests arrived in the evening the Mother Superior gave every child their specially marked present from the tree. Lists were made weeks in advance for, as the account reminded readers, 'If you only expect one present during the year, it makes a great difference if that one is what you most want.'

Figure 129 *Sister Cynthia Clare on her profession in 1971.*

After the Sisters received their gifts there was a special party supper with the 'unknown luxury' of sandwiches and blancmange. The following evening the tree was moved to the embroidery workroom and re-decorated for a present-giving tea party for 200 members of the Mothers' Guild and Girls' Guild. Students from the night school came the next night for their celebrations. [208]

Today, Christmas for residents of the Old Convent begins with the annual carol concert, now in its twentieth year. Accompanied by the Croydon Salvation Army Brass Band, residents and their guests fill the usually empty space with joyful music. The fact that everyone has to dress up warmly in coats and gloves to combat the lack of heating simply adds to the wintry atmosphere, making the supply of mulled wine and mince pies all the more welcome. Over the years this event has raised thousands of pounds for charity.

The Old Convent remains a special place and though its use has changed it is still much loved by the people who once lived there and by those who call it home today. The legacy of the women who gave their lives to it and to everything it stood for is a truly inspiring one for it extends across the globe and down through generations. To those women this book is dedicated.

Timeline

1845   Creation of the first Anglican Sisterhood

1846   John Mason Neale takes up the post of Warden at Sackville College, East Grinstead

1854   The first four recruits join Neale's Sisterhood

1855   Ann Gream is professed as first Mother Superior of the Sisterhood of St Margaret. The Sisters begin nursing at Rotherfield

1856   The Sisterhood leases No. 8 Church Lane, East Grinstead

1857   The orphanage comes to East Grinstead from Brighton
After Sister Amy dies of scarlet fever there are riots at her funeral in Lewes

1858   The Sisters move to No. 1 Church Lane

1862   St Agnes' School is established to educate the daughters of gentlemen

1864   Land is purchased for a new convent off Moat Road and G E Street prepares the first plans

1865   The foundation stone of the convent is laid on St Margaret's Day, 20 July

1866   John Mason Neale dies on 6 August, aged 48

1870   The first convent buildings are opened

1883   The chapel is opened

1895   St Margaret's College opens for the daughters of local families

1902   Mother Alice dies after 38 years as Superior. She is succeeded by Mother Ermenild

1908   The extension of St Agnes' School is completed

1917   St Margaret's College becomes St Michael's College

1933   The two schools of St Agnes' and St Michael's join together

1972   The Sisters move out of the convent and work begins on a new, smaller building.

        The Victorian buildings are Grade II* listed and are taken over by the school which merges with Kingsley School from Horley to become Kingsley St Michael.

1976   The school closes and the convent is sold

1978   The first residents move into the old convent

2020   150th Anniversary of the Convent's opening

Notes

Introduction

1 Littledale, *Guardian* obituary
2 Williamson, p357
3 Anson, p337

Chapter 1 The Society of St Margaret

4 Shelton Reed, p213
5 Quoted in Mumm, p4
6 Mumm, p3
7 Mother Kate, p13
8 Lough, p14
9 Drain, p2
10 Neale wrote an account of the riot which he addressed 'To the Inhabitants of East Grinstead,' quoted in Lough, pp86-7
11 Mother Kate, p15
12 Mother Kate, pp14-15
13 Neale, *Sermons*, p368
14 Mitton, p25
15 Letter to Benjamin Webb, 1 Feb 1855 in Lawson, p233
16 Ibid, p234-5
17 Letter to Joseph Haskoll, 13 March 1855 in Lawson, p236. Haskoll was Neale's friend and literary executor. He died in 1871
18 Sackville list. Sister Miriam referred to Sister Elizabeth in the SMHYC, July 1900, p222
19 Letter to Webb, 1 Feb 1855 in Lawson, p234
20 Ibid, p236
21 Letter to Webb, 14 April 1855 in Lawson, p238
22 Lawson, p271
23 *Doing the Impossible*, p14
24 Anson, p337, note 1 regarding the history of Reservation in Anglican churches
25 Mother Kate, p35
26 *Doing the Impossible*, pp14-15
27 Lough, pp106-7
28 SMM, Vol IV No 15, July 1894, p109
29 Ibid, p115
30 'A Letter to the Revd. John M. Neale by the Revd. John Scobell', *Sussex Advertiser and Officer*, p3. Quoted in Lough, p108. The Sisterhood Rules subsequently clarified the position on legacies from serving Sisters 'To prevent all possible mistakes and unworthy suspicions, any bequest made by a Sister; for the benefit of S. Margaret's, if dated less than six calends months before her death, will not be accepted without the written consent of the heir-at-law. If that consent be not given, the sum thus bequeathed will be handed over to some other Charity.' Wakeling, 1871, p9

31 Letter to Webb, 7 December 1857 in Lawson, p299; Lough, p112

32 Mother Kate, pp21-2

33 Ibid, pp21-2

34 Bodley's design for the cross was assessed in *The Ecclesiologist*, No CXXVIII, October 1858, p347

35 Lawson, p335

36 Mother Kate, pp28-9. This may have been inspired by the example of Priscilla Lydia Sellon's Sisters of the Holy Trinity. They had printing presses in their houses at Devonport and Bristol (later Bradford on Avon), one of which was a gift from Pusey. The Sisters used their presses to train girls as compositors so that they could earn higher wages than if they became servants. My thanks to Ivor Slocombe for this information

37 Mother Kate, p6

38 'Memory of over forty years ago' by Mother Kate, SMHYC, July 1904, pp220-2

Chapter 2 A Purpose-built Convent

39 *Doing the Impossible*, p24

40 Letter to Haskoll, 19 August 1864 in Lawson, pp343-4

41 Quoted in White, p11

42 Chandler, p30

43 Quoted in White, p3

44 Ibid, p4

45 Ibid, p41

46 Scott, p88

47 Ibid, p88

48 White, p46

49 Hall, p24

50 Chandler, p37

51 A E Street, *Memoir of George Edmund Street*, p56

52 A E Street, p20

53 A E Street, p17

54 Drawings at Lambeth Palace Library, CM29, 3 items

55 SMM, Vol III, No 13, July 1893, p311

56 Atkins, pp2-3; Leppard p7

57 Anson, p336

58 *The Ecclesiologist*, No CLXXVI, October 1866, p266

59 Goodhart-Rendel, p12

60 'A Visit to East Grinstead', dated Nov 1865, no publication information. Pusey House Library, Box 6, 137 - Press Cuttings

61 A E Street, p50

62 Letter to Haskoll, 19 August 1864 in Lawson, pp344

63 A E Street, p84

64 Brownlee, *DNB*; Hitchcock, p151; A E Street, p20

65 Eastlake, p323

66 Hitchcock, p152

67 Hitchcock, p153

68 *Church Review*, 22 July 1865, Pusey House Library, Box 6, 137 - Press Cuttings

69 *Guardian*, 26 July, 1865, Pusey House Library, Box 6, 137 - Press Cuttings

70 SMM, Vol IV, No.17, July 1895, p362. A later reference proves that if Neale had been exonerated in East Grinstead he was still unwelcome elsewhere. In a letter to Haskoll of 15 February 1866 he mentioned being mobbed in Liverpool by people who shouted out '"Who murdered Miss Scobell?" etc.etc.' Lawson, p363

71 SMM, Vol IV, No.17, July 1895, p352

72 *Guardian*, 26 July, 1865, Pusey House Library, Box 6, 137 - Press Cuttings

73 *Sussex Express*, 25 July 1865, Pusey House Library, Box 6, 137 - Press Cuttings

Chapter 3 The Progress of Works

74 SMM, July 1895, p354-5

75 'To the Workmen of St Margaret's College,' dated 16 July 1866, Pusey House, Box 6, 137 press cuttings

76 Letter to Haskoll, Feast of S Hilary 1866 in SMM, July 1895, p355

77 Littledale obituary

78 *Ecclesiologist*, 1866, pp265

79 CT, 18 August 1866, p1

80 SMM, July 1895, pp361-2

81 CT, 18 August 1866, p1

82 Hills, p213

83 Mother Alice' obituary by Mother Kate, SMHYC, July 1902, p40

84 Ibid, p42

85 CT, 22 July 1870, p326

86 A E Street, p136

87 CT, 22 July 1870, p326

88 ILN, 20 June 1868, p618

89 Letter from Hugh Meller, The Victorian Society, 27 January 1978. Michael Leppard Collection/The Author

90 Anson, p336

91 RIBA drawing PA 157/4/20. This altar was later split in two with one half used in the sacristy and the other half sent to the daughter house in Colombo, Sri Lanka. Pusey House, Box 57, 82 Black exercise book

92 Hugh Meller letter op cit

93 SMM, July 1889, p458. Black exercise book, Pusey House Box 57, 82. In 1925 this window was found to be in poor repair 'Mr Street carried out all the mullions and tracery in the local stone, which has proved unsuitable; it needs repointing and repairing, both inside and out, to save the window, which is one of the best we have.' SMHYC, July 1925, p280

94 SMHYC, July 1904, p228

95 1998 Presentation, Pusey House

96 Ibid

97 Ibid; RIBA drawing PA157/4/19; In 1910 plans were made to update the laundry but the funds had to be diverted to other maintenance work

98 Wakeling, pp15, 20

99 Goodhart-Rendel, p13. Though Shaw had left Street's office in 1862 he was, coincidentally, working at Hammerwood just outside East Grinstead in 1872 building a school and school house

100 Pusey House, Box 6, 137 Press cuttings

101 Lawson, p360

102 Lawson, p362

103 *Bradford Observer*, June 23 1864, Pusey House, Box 6, 137 press cuttings

104 *Staffordshire Advertiser*, 22 Aug 1864, Pusey House, Box 6, 137 press cuttings

105 Letter to Haskoll 8 Dec 1862, SMM, Vol IV, No 17, July 1895, pp332-3

106 'Mother Ann's Journal of begging tours 1866-7', Pusey House, Box 55

107 Ibid

108 CT, 22 July 1870, p326

109 1998 Presentation, Pusey House

110 At her death in 1894 Charlotte Rosa Raine owned houses in Oxfordshire, Brighton and the Isle of Wight. In her will she left £1000 to the Sisters of St Margaret. She also made provision for the continuing care of her cats, eight of which were individually named. 'An Eccentric Will', ILN, 29 September 1894, p398

111 AE Street, p130-31

112 AE Street, p271

113 CT, 23 Dec 1881, p887

114 AE Street, p277; SMHYC, 20 July 1911, p131

115 Williamson, p358

116 Anson, p336

117 This information comes from a handwritten history in a black exercise book, Pusey House, Box 57, 82

118 Williamson, p358

119 Williamson, p358; black exercise book, Pusey House, Box 57, 81; Official Guide 1909, Pusey House, Box 57, 81

120 Hills, p212

121 Lough, p83

122 SMHYC, Jan 1904, p168

123 SMHYC, July 1905, p299

124 SMHYC, Jan 1926, p3

125 *Building News*, 13 June 1890, p830

126 A E Street - Biographical File, RIBA Library

127 SMHYC, July 1903, p129

128 J C Stockdale - Biographical File, RIBA Library

Chapter 4 Convent Life

129 www.theweald.org/P2.asp?PId=EG.StMCon

130 Quoted in Anson, p433, taken from *The Church and the World*, ed Rev Orby Shipley, London 1867, pp184-7

131 Anson, pp433-4

132 Mumm, p87; p68

133 Spencer, p13

134 Mother Kate, p223

135 Chandler, p86

136 CT, 22 July 1870, p326. My thanks to Caroline Metcalfe for the additional information about the workman. Sister Elizabeth died 29 August 1860 (see p25); Sister Emma was professed on 28 March 1861 and died 24 October 1862

137 SMHYC, July 1902, pp45-6

138 *Doing the Impossible*, p48

139 Letter to Webb, 23 May 1855 in Lawson, p239

140 SMM, Jan 1895, p310; Littledale obituary

141 SMM, Jan 1894, pp16-17

142 'A Visit to East Grinstead', dated Nov 1865, no publication information. Pusey House Library, Box 6, 137 - Press Cuttings

143 *Doing the Impossible*, p25-6

144 SMM, Vol. 1, July 1887, p42

145 *Doing the Impossible*, pp35-6

146 *Doing the Impossible*, p36; 1998 Presentation, Pusey House

147 *Doing the Impossible*, p50; SMHYC, Jan 1915, pp84-5. The soldiers only stayed a short time before being moved on to Haywards Heath

148 SMHYC, Jan 1917, p233

149 Sister Catherine Louise, pp115-6

150 Doing the Impossible, p22, p20

151 Hills, p211. He left out the mission at Scarborough established in 1900. The Sisters work was so broad and changing that it can be hard to keep track of every misison. A good overview can be found in the book by Sister Catherine Louise

152 *Doing the Impossible*, p34

153 For a fuller account of the Sister's foreign missions see Chapter 7 of Doing the Impossible (pp36-43)

154 Wakeling, 1871, p10

155 1998 Presentation, Pusey House

156 SMHYC, Jan 1907, pp61-63. Christina Sedding also joined St Margaret's and is recorded there in the 1881 census

157 CT, 22 July 1870, p326

158 Schoeser, p47

159 Schoeser, p114. Wakeling noted in 1871 that William Burges was also among the architects to 'have kindly promised their assistance'

160 My thanks to Sarah Sexton for this information

161 SMM, July 1887, p41

162 Humphreys, p118

163 Schoeser, p115

164 CT, 17 Dec 1869, p502

165 SMHYC, July 1903, pp131-2

166 *Doing the Impossible*, p32

167 SMHYC, July 1911, pp128-31

168 Schoeser, p96

169 CT, 28 July 1905, p113

Chapter 5 The Orphanage and Schools

170 SMM, Jan 1894, pp21-2

171 My thanks to Tom Scratchley for this information

172 1998 Presentation, Pusey House

173 SMM, Jan 1888, p114

174 Ibid., pp114-5

175 Ibid., pp79-80

176 Spencer, pp 11-12

177 SMHYC, July 1902, pp48-9

178 Spencer, p14

179 1998 Presentation, Pusey House; Sackville College list; 1881 census return www.theweald.org/P2.asp?PId=EG.StMCon

180 SMHYC, Jan 1903, pp79-80

181 SMHYC, July 1906, pp68-9

182 SMHYC, July 1911, p125

183 *Doing the Impossible*, p53

184 Mother Kate, p82

185 see Lawson, pp 273, 275-6

186 Lawson, p303; Mother Kate, pp26-7

187 SMHYC, Jan 1924, p179; Sister Miriam was the granddaughter of popular Victorian painter Alfred Nicholson. Sister Kate who knew her from 1858, when both began their connection with St Margaret's, described her as 'a good linguist and a brilliant scholar'. After Neale's death and the passing of his literary executor Joseph Haskoll, it was Sister Miriam who prepared his works for publication and produced the memoir that appeared in the SMM from 1887. SMHYC, July 1909, pp221-2; letter to Haskoll 8 Dec 1862 in Lawson p341. See p25 re Sister Elizabeth

188 SMHYC, July 1909, pp222

189 Lawson, p341

190 Lawson, p344

191 SMHYC, July 1909, pp222; handwritten notes on Moat Road in Box 32 St Michael's School, Pusey House

192 SMHYC, Jan 1903, p81

193 SMHYC, July 1905, p302

194 SMHYC, July 1907, p90

195 SMHYC, Jan 1907, p60

196 SMHYC, July 1918, p40

197 SMHYC, Jan 1924, p187

198 SMHYC, Jan 1927 p83

199 Sister Catherine Louise, p47

200 *Doing the Impossible*, p51

201 1962 press cutting from unknown publication in Box 32, 164 'Centenary Scrapbook, St Agnes later St Michael's', Pusey House

202 *Doing the Impossible*, pp57-8

203 *Doing the Impossible*, p59

204 'Death of a School', East Grinstead Observer, 11 August 1976 in Box 32, 164 'Centenary Scrapbook, St Agnes later St Michael's', Pusey House

205 Hugh Meller letter, 27 Jan 1978, p2

Chapter 6 Change and Legacy

206 Sister Sarah SSM, St Mary's and St Margaret's December 2016 Newsletter, p17 www.saintmarysconventchiswick.org/uploads/5/2/1/8/521848/newsletter_dec_2016__final_.pdf Mother Kate, quoted in Schoeser, p94

207 Mumm, pp9-10

208 SMM, July 1889, pp437-443

Bibliography

Archives

~ SSM Archives, Pusey House Library, Oxford
Including '1998 Presentation' – original handwritten script in two parts catalogued as Box 73, 301 'Presentation of early history, 1855-80' produced for the 1998 Open Day as a 'dramatisation of the facts based on early diaries', unpaginated

~ Sackville College Library – handwritten list of Sisters (cited as Sackville College list)

~ Lambeth Palace Library, Neale Papers

~ Michael Leppard Collection of papers on SSM (now with the author)

~ Paul Joyce Collection on G E Street at the Paul Mellon Centre, London

~ Royal Institute of British Architects (RIBA) Library

~ RIBA Drawings Collection at the V&A – PA157/4 (1-36), PA157/4 (37-40)

Periodicals

~ *Building News*

~ CT – *Church Times*

~ *The Ecclesiologist*

~ ILN – *Illustrated London News*

~ SMM – *St Margaret's Magazine*, East Grinstead 1887-1901

~ SMHYC – *St Margaret's Half-Yearly Chronicle*, East Grinstead, 1902-1975

~ SMC – *St Margaret's Chronicle*, East Grinstead, 1976-1995

Books and articles

~ Anson, Peter F., *The Call of the Cloister: Religious Communities and kindred bodies in the Anglican Communion*, London, 1955

~ Atkins, Keith 'The Cottage Hospital Movement in England & Wales 1850 -1914: Origins, Growth and Contribution to the Healthcare of the Poor', unpublished PhD thesis, Kingston University, December 2018 https://eprints.kingston.ac.uk/43861/

~ Brownlee, David B, 'George Edmund Street', *Oxford Dictionary of National Biography*, 2008 (online edition)

~ Chandler, Michael, *The Life and Work of John Mason Neale, 1818-1866*, Gracewing Books, 1995

~ *Doing the Impossible; A short historical sketch of St. Margaret's Convent, East Grinstead 1855-1980 (with Postscript 2000)* by a Sister of the Society (S. Gabriel)

~ Drain, Susan, 'John Mason Neale', *Oxford Dictionary of National Biography*, 2014

~ Eastlake, Charles, *A History of the Gothic Revival*, London, 1872

~ Ferry, Kathryn, 'A sea of gables: The Old Convent, East Grinstead, West Sussex', Country Life, 4 November 2020, pp66-72
'Statement of Significance for Corrugated Iron Building to the rear of Church Lane, East Grinstead,' unpublished report, 2015

~ Goodhart-Rendel, H.S. 'George Edmund Street', *Transactions of the Ecclesiological Society*, 1953 (reprinted as a booklet, 1983)

~ Hall, Michael, *George Frederick Bodley and the later Gothic Revival in Britain and America*, Yale University Press, 2014

~ Hills, Wallace H. *The Illustrated History of East Grinstead*, (2016 facsimile of 1906 edition)

- Hitchcock, Henry-Russell, 'G E Street in the 1850s,' *Journal of the Society of Architectural Historians*, Vol. 19, No. 4 (Dec., 1960), pp145-171

- Howarth, Janet, 'The Church of England and Women's Higher Education c1840-1914' in *Politics and Culture in Victorian Britain: Essays in Memory of Colin Matthew*, eds Peter Ghash and Lawrence Goldman, Oxford, 2006, chapter 10

- Humphreys, Mary Gay, 'Art Needlework', *The Art Amateur*, Vol. 5, No. 6 (Nov 1881) pp118-120

- Lawson, Mary Sackville (ed), *Letters of John Mason Neale, D.D.,* 1910

- Leppard, M. J., 'The pre-history of cottage hospitals', *Bulletin 437*, Surrey Archaeological Society, February 2013, pp7-8

- Littledale, R F, 'John Mason Neale' (obituary notice) *The Guardian*, August 15, 1866

- Lough, A. G., *John Mason Neale: Priest Extraordinary*, Privately published, 1975

- Mitton, Lavinia *The Victorian Hospital*, Shire Publications, 2008

- Mother Kate, S.S.M. *Memories of a Sister of St. Saviour's Priory*, A R Mowbray & Co Ltd, 1903

- Mumm, Susan, *Stolen Daughters, Virgin Mothers: Anglican Sisterhoods in Victorian Britain,* Leicester University Press, 1999

- Neale, John Mason, *Sermons on the Song of Songs, preached in the Oratory of St Margaret's, East Grinstead*, 1867 https://babel.hathitrust.org/cgi/pt?id=uc1.31175026790116&view=1up&seq=391 retrieved 15 Oct 2019

- Quekett, Edward, 'St Margaret's Convent, East Grinstead', unpublished BA dissertation, University of Cambridge, 2012

- Reed, John Shelton, "A Female Movement": The Feminization of Nineteenth Century Anglo-Catholicism', *Anglican and Episcopal History*, Vol 57, No 2 (June 1988) pp199-238

- Schoeser, Mary, *English Church Embroidery 1833-1953*, Watts & Co. Ltd in association with the Friends of Liverpool Cathedral Embroidery Museum, 2nd ed 1998

- Scott, G G, *Personal and Professional Recollections by the late Sir George Gilbert Scott edited by his son G. Gilbert Scott*, London, 1879

- Sister Catherine Louise, S.S.M. *The Planting of the Lord: The History of the Society of Saint Margaret in England, Scotland and the U.S.A. 1855-1995*, privately printed

- Sister Miriam, S.S.M. 'John Mason Neale: A Memoir', series of articles in St. Margaret's Magazine, 1887-96 (these were also published together in 1903)

- Spencer, Sylvia and Joan Sankey, *Convent Memories*, The Book Guild Ltd, 1997

- Street, Arthur Edmund, *Memoir of George Edmund Street, 1824-1881*, John Murray, 1881 (facsimile)

- Wakeling, G., *St. Margaret's, East Grinstead, Sussex*, Brighton, 1871 http://anglican history.org/religious/east_grinsted1871.html retrieved 25 Feb 2020

- White, James F. *The Cambridge Movement: The Ecclesiologists and the Gothic Revival*, Cambridge University Press, 1962

- Williamson, E., Hudson, T. Musson J. and Nairn I., *The Buildings of England: Sussex: West,* New Haven & London, 2019

Webpages

- What was the Oxford Movement www.puseyhouse.org.uk/what-was-the-oxford-movement.html

- The people who built Brighton and Hove: F – John Fabian www.brightonhistory.org.uk/architects/architects_f.html

- Bell and Beckham stained glass commissions www.victorianweb.org/art/stainedglass/bellandbeckham/index.html

- Bloomsbury project re Queen Square, London www.ucl.ac.uk/bloomsbury-project/articles/events/Queen%20Square.pdf

- Census returns retrieved www.theweald.org/P2.asp?PId=EG.StMCon

- Wikipedia on SSM en.wikipedia.org/wiki/Society_of_Saint_Margaret

- Mother Kate biography anglicanhistory.org/bios/motherkate.html

- John Mason Neale gravestone www.metcas.me.uk/steves-home-page/carolines-historical-notes/st-swithuns-articles/04-the-memorial-and-grave-of-john-mason-neale/

Picture credits

Cover illustration and 74, 124 by Susan Quekett; 1, 19, 58, 61, 63, 66, 81, 82, 91, 123 Will Pryce / Country Life; 2, 8, 11, 72, 73, 83, 84, 88, 122 East Grinstead Museum; 3, 15, 17, 18, 20, 32, 33, 36, 47, 48, 50, 53, 57, 64, 70, 71, 75, 76, 77, 78, 87, 90, 94, 95, 96, 98, 99, 100, 101, 102, 103, 104, 105, 106, 107, 108, 110, 111, 112, 113, 114, 115, 116, 117, 120, 121, 128, 129 By kind permission of The Principal and Chapter of Pusey House / The Society of St Margaret; 4 Caroline and Steve Metcalfe; 5 Ivor Slocombe Collection; 6, 12, 40, 62, 85, 86 SSM Magazines by kind permission of the Trustees of Sackville College; 7, 14, 39, 51, 79 Will Pryce / TOCERL; 9, 24, 34, 38, 56, 80 Francis Barchard Photograph Album © Victoria & Albert Museum, London; 10, 25, 27, 42, 43, 44, 45, 46, 49, 65, 67, 97, 109, 127 Author; 13, 16, 35, 68, 118, 119, 125, 126, 128 Author/Michael Leppard Collection; 21 Will Quekett; 22 Richard Mammana http://anglicanhistory.org/england/crake_deformation/; 23 Creative Commons/Photo by DAVID ILIFF. License: CC BY-SA 3.0; 26 Dr Alex Bremner; 28 Ned Quekett; 29 Bloxham School; 30 Society for the Protection of Ancient Monuments; 31 Creative Commons / Saffron Blaze via https://www.mackenzie.co; 37, 54, 55, 59, 60 RIBA Collection; 41, 52, 93 Paul Joyce Collection / Paul Mellon Centre for British Art; 69 © Chapter of York: Reproduced by kind permission; 89 Susan Quekett / With thanks to the Dean & Chapter of Chichester Cathedral; 92 By kind permission of Liverpool Cathedral

Index

Aldershot 121, 127

Alison, Laughton 101, 102, 103

All Saints, Margaret Street, Westminster 47, 49, 52, 144

All Saints, Selsey, Glos 61

Anglican Sisterhoods: 15, 22, 25, 131, 158, 177; All Saints (Marylebone) 17; Holy Cross (Park Village) 16; Holy Cross (Haywards Heath) 34; Most Holy Trinity (Ascot Priory) 16; Saint Mary the Virgin (Wantage) 17, 52, 57

Arts and Crafts Movement 57, 108, 132, 136, 164, 178, 179

Ashdown Forest 22, 79

Ashurst Wood 37, 56

Barchard, Francis 63, 64, 65, 71, 98

Beaulieu Abbey, Hampshire 80

Belgian refugees 124

Benham & Sons, Wigmore Street 83

Bell & Beckham 80, 103

Betjeman, John 141

Beyreuth Festival 156

Bishop of Chichester 20, 33, 42, 65, 131, 139, 141, 163

Bloxham School, Banbury 57-9, 67

Bodley, George Frederick 26, 29, 33, 35, 49, 51, 60, 61, 70, 71, 98, 136

Boer War 128, 155

Boston Children's Hospital, 127-8

Boyce, Edward 19, 20, 46, 48

Boyd, Pattie 167

Brighton 20, 34, 61, 63, 70, 144, 162: Churches: St Mary the Virgin & St Mary Magdelene 70;

St Michael & All Angels 70, 71; St Paul's 38, 70, 144: St Mary's Sisterhood 25

Buckingham Palace, London 139

Butler, William John 17, 52, 57

Butterfield, William 47, 49, 131, 170

Byron, Harriet Brownlow 17

Cambridge 20, 46, 48, 103, 161: Colleges: Downing 20; Girton 38; Newnham 38, 168; Trinity 19

Cambridge Camden Society (CCS) 14, 20, 43, 46, 48, 49, 50, 54, 131, 179

Carter, Owen Browne 50

Catholic Emancipation Act, 1929 9, 14

Clewer, Community of St John the Baptist 17, 24, 39, 117, 170; St Stephen's School 158

Comper, John 43, 127

Cottage hospital 29, 53, 55, 60, 122, 127

Cottage nursing 25, 27, 120-1, 122, 124: Epidemics 121

Crawley, West Sussex 20, 46, 122

Crimean War 24, 27

Crystal Palace, Sydenham 145

Cuddesdon Theological College 57, 58, 81

Day, Harriet 17

De la Warr, Earl and Lady 20, 141

Earp, Thomas 76, 95, 101

East Grinstead: Cemetery, West Hill 118; Church Lane 12, 26, 29, 31, 33, 34, 35, 37, 51, 65, 73, 130, 144, 158; London Road 35, 43, 144, 161; Moat Road 9, 35, 36, 51, 56, 65, 148, 159, 161, 162, 165, 166, 168, 174, 175: Pubs: Crown Inn 66; Dorset Arms 38; Ship Inn 35, 37; St Swithun's Church 15, 30, 72, 118, 174: Queen Victoria Hospital 125, 174

Ecclesiological Society, see also the Cambridge Camden Society 20, 49, 51, 52, 54-5

Ecclesiologist, The 48, 49, 55, 60, 73

Embroidery: Commissions 38, 130, 138: Chichester Cathedral 131, 139; Coronation chairs of Estate, 1911 139; St Mary the Virgin, New York 137, 139; St Paul's Cathedral 137; York Minster 108, 133: School 136-7: Exhibition 1959 140-1

Fabian, John 70-2

Gilbert and Sullivan 167

Gothic Revival 9,10, 43, 46, 49, 57

Gream, Ann (see also Mother Ann) 23, 25

Gream, Katherine 25, 70

Hackenden quarry, East Grinstead 56, 70, 104, 152

Haskoll, Joseph 43, 70, 90

Herbert, Sidney, 1st Baron Herbert of Lea 27

Hitler, Adolf 156

Hooke Hall, Uckfield 176

Hutton, Reginald 103

Industrials (see also St Lucy's) 83, 115, 116, 129, 152, 153

Joyce, Paul 84-5

Leaver, James 76-7

Lewes, East Sussex 31, 121: Lewes Riot 32, 38, 158

McIndoe, Archibald 125

Medland, John 137

Monsell, Harriet 17

Morris, William 57, 133, 178: Morris & Co. 136, 139

Merthyr Tydfil, Wales 121, 127

National Trust, The 178

Navvies 38, 73

Neale, Elizabeth 34, 144

Neale, John Mason: architectural ideas 43, 48, 51-3, 55, 60, 66, 164, 178-9; as teacher 75, 177; at Cambridge 14, 19, 48; charitable works 37, 38; death 65, 72-3, 75, 93, 103, 118; educational enterprises 158-61; founder of SSM 8, 9, 10, 23-9, 61, 110, 117, 119-20, 129, 139, 177; fundraising 90, 92, 158; inhibition from preaching 20, 42; literary work 20, 22, 46, 116; mission work 125, 127, 128; orphanage 144-6; relationship with workmen 70; reputation 23, 32, 61, 63, 73, 103; riots against 23, 32, 63; religious ideas 29, 30, 45, 46, 162; vestments 130-2; Warden of Sackville College 18, 20-2, 48, 103; youth 18-20

Neale, Katherine Ermenild see SSM Superiors: Mother Ermenild

Neale, Sarah (neé Webster) 20

Neale House, East Grinstead 174-5

Nightingale, Florence 23, 27, 119

Norman & Burt, Burgess Hill 164

Oxford 23, 51, 57; St Anne's School, Rewley House 158

Oxford Movement 9, 14, 15, 43, 46, 65, 70, 131: Keble, John 14: Newman, Henry 14: Pusey, Edmund 14, 16

Philadelphia Worlds Fair, 1876 136

Pugin, Augustus Welby Northmore 43-4, 45, 46, 48, 60, 131

Pulborough, West Sussex 120

Raine, Charlotte Rosa 93

Rossetti, Dante Gabriel 133

Rotherfield, East Sussex 24, 25, 27, 29, 65

Royal Courts of Justice, London 100, 106

Sackville College, East Grinstead 18, 19, 20, 21, 22, 24, 25, 26, 30, 33, 35, 48, 49, 52, 61, 73, 103, 139, 141, 144, 174

Scobell, Emily (Sister Amy) 30-2, 35, 65

Scobell, John 30-2

Scott, George Gilbert 29, 48-9, 50-1, 55, 76, 137

Scott, Sir Walter 46, 79

Sedding, Edmund 57, 63, 133, 178

Sedding, John Dando 57, 63, 108, 133, 178

Sellon, Priscilla Lydia 17

Shaw, Richard Norman 57, 87, 178

Shoreham, West Sussex 119-20, 122

Smith, Kenneth 169, 171

Southey, Robert 15

Spencer, Stanley 148

Spencer, Sylvia 116, 148-51, 153, 156

St Augustine's, Bristol 61

St Catherine's Home, Ventnor 117, 127

St John's House, East Grinstead 124, 138, 162, 165, 167, 175

St Katherine's, Queen Square, London 136-7

St Lucy's House (see also Industrials) 116, 152 ,153, 168

St Margaret of Antioch 25, 70

St Margaret's Convent: wafer bakery 137-8, 139, 162, 175; cemetery 94, 117-9, 174; chapel 8, 11, 61, 65, 67, 77, 78, 79, 80, 82, 93, 95-104, 107, 114, 118, 129, 133, 136, 161, 164,166, 167, 171, 172, 174; chaplain's lodge 86, 87, 88; embroidery workroom 83, 86, 87, 95, 123, 131, 132, 133, 134, 139, 141, 178, 181; gardens 115, 116; guest house 65, 86, 94, 95, 96-7, 104-5, 107; infirmary 65, 95, 100, 117, 123, 124; laundry 72, 75, 83, 86, 106, 112, 124; lodge 77, 86, 87, 123; kitchen 65, 67, 72, 75, 77, 78, 79, 82, 106, 115, 116, 118, 152, 153, 168, 170; refectory 72, 74, 75, 79-80, 104, 116, 118, 125, 133, 136, 140-1, 151, 153, 164, 180

St Margaret's Home (see also East Grinstead: Church Lane) 12, 33, 35, 36, 51, 73, 80

St Margaret's Needlework Society 127

St Margaret's Orphanage 34, 36, 63, 65, 75, 89, 90, 116, 125, 126, 130, 132, 138, 141, 142, 144-56, 157, 158, 160, 162, 166, 179

Society of St Margaret (SSM) Associates 93, 102, 105, 117, 138, 147

SSM Houses 119: Aberdeen, Scotland 43, 127; Boston, Massachusetts 127-8, 176; Colombo, Sri Lanka 113, 128, 129, 176; Priory of the Holy Cross, Haggerston 116, 126, 176; Johannesburg, South Africa 127, 128, 129; St Mary's Convent, Chiswick 127, 176; Priory of Our Lady, Walsingham 176

SSM Missions 125-7: Cardiff, Glamorgan 127; Hitchin, Herts 121, 127; East Grinstead (Parish Works) 128-9; Frome, Somerset 127, 153; St Mary's, Soho 63, 125-6, 128, 133, 145

SSM Schools: St Agnes' 35, 36, 61, 65, 87, 101, 107, 132, 138, 151, 156, 157, 158, 159, 160-7, 169, 170; St Agnes' and St Michael's 157, 163, 166, 167, 169, 170, 176; St Margaret's College 156, 165, 166; St Michael's 157, 159, 165,166; Kingsley St Michael 169-70

SSM Sisters: Sr Ada 153; Sr Alice (see Mother Alice); Sr Alma Mary 176; Sr Amy (see Scobell, Emily); Sr Christina 178; Sr Cynthia Clare 181; Sr Dominica 82; Sr Edith 101, 103-4, 141; Sr Edna 118; Sr Eleanor, 119; Sr Elizabeth 25, 160; Sr Ellen 24, 27, 119, 120, 160; Sr Elsa 115, 124; Sr Evelyn 93; Sr Frances 39; Sr Grace Margaret 129; Sr Gertrude 39, 128-9; Sr Isa 39, 132, 133-6; Sr Isabel 37; Sr Jane 144; Sr Joan Margaret 174; Sr Kate (later Mother Kate) 18, 22, 30, 33, 38, 75, 82, 116, 126, 133, 145, 157, 158, 176, 177; Sr Lucy 39, 91, 119; Sr Maria 93, 124;

Sr Mary 132, 145; Sr Mary Joan 174; Sr Miriam 121, 128, 153, 158-60; Sr Sarah 176; Sr Susannah 161; Sr Theresa 127-8; Sr Winifred 137; Sr Zillah 93, 132

SSM Superiors 24-5, 63, 65, 87, 106, 110, 113-4, 117, 119, 180: Mother Alice 25, 27, 39, 73, 75, 80, 82, 92, 93, 105, 114, 117, 118, 127, 128, 132, 162; Mother Ann 23, 24, 25, 29, 30, 32, 33, 35, 65, 70, 75, 91-3, 101, 114, 118, 144, 153; Mother Ermenild 39, 114, 117, 123-5, 127, 175; Mother Gabriel 29, 114, 124, 138, 156, 166, 169; Mother Geraldine Mary 114; Mother Hazel 169; Mother Madeleine 112, 114, 157, 166

Standen, East Grinstead 178-9

Stockdale, John Carrington 106, 163-4

Street, Arthur Edmund 57, 76, 100, 104-6, 152, 162, 165

Street, George Edmund 10, 29, 43, 49, 50-4, 55, 56, 57, 58, 59, 60, 61, 66, 68, 70, 76, 79, 80, 81, 82, 84, 87, 88-9, 94, 95, 96-7, 98, 100, 101, 104-5, 106, 118, 125, 130, 131, 133, 134, 135, 136, 161, 164, 166, 170, 175, 178

Thomson, Dr Spencer 55

Tunbridge Wells, Kent 27, 37, 127

Victorian Society, The 79, 170

Wagner, Arthur Douglas 70, 72

Wagner, Henry Michell 38, 70

Wagner, Winifred 155-6

Wall & Hook, Brimscombe, Glos 96, 98, 104

Wantage, Berks 17, 51, 52, 57

Warburton, Katherine Anne Egerton (see also SSM Sister Kate) 33

Webb, Benjamin 20, 29, 38, 46, 48, 158

Webb, Geoffrey 136

Webb, Philip 57, 60, 178-9

Westminster Hospital, London 24, 119

White, William 49, 51

Wilberforce, Samuel 57

Woodyer, Henry 170

World War I 124, 125, 164

World War II 125, 129, 153, 156

Portraits painted on glass from windows in the cloister

George Edmund Street RA
14 Cavendish Place W
Sep.r 1871.

George Edmund Street RA
14 Cavendish Place W
Sep.r 1871.

is one of the nineteen drawings referred to in the
act signed by us this fifteenth day of
in the year of our Lord one thousand eight
hundred and seventy one.